SURREY

IN THE SIXTIES

Memories of a swinging decade

by Mark Davison and Ian Currie

Surrey was swinging in the Sixties along with the rest of Britain. Dance halls were packed with teenagers raving to the records that hurtled up the hit parade to become all-time golden greats in the years that followed. But despite the creative explosion in the music and fashion world, these were times of terrible tragedy for Surrey's olde worlde towns. Quaint little shops and cottages were barged out of the way by bulldozers making way for concrete jungles.

Flick through the pages and re-live the days of bouffant hair styles, winklepickers, bubble cars, Zodiacs and trolleybuses.

FROSTED EARTH

An advert from the Woking News and Mail in February 1960. Feeling hungry?

ISBN 0-9516710-4-9

First edition November 1994
Reprinted December 1994
Reprinted December 1996
Reprinted November 1998
Reprinted July 2004

Published by Mark Davison, North Bank, Smoke Lane, Reigate, Surrey RH2 7HJ

Tel 01737 221215

e-mail: mark.davison1@virgin.net

Printed by *Litho Techniques (Kenley) Ltd,*
46-50 Godstone Road, Whyteleafe,
Surrey CR3 0EA
www.lithotechniques.com

Fonts *Bodoni and Times*

Acknowledgements

Gladys Arlett and Dorking museum staff; Greta Morley; Maureen Lewington; Chris Porter; Andrew Wills; Jeremy Harte, Bourne Hall Museum; John Janaway, Duncan and staff at Surrey Local Studies Library; Philip Butler, Ash; Graham Wootten, BT Museum; Paul Gunner; Brian and Jill Bailey of Addlestone; Ian Wakeford of Old Woking; Woking Library staff; Jackie Everett, and staff at Jackman's Woking; Paul and Roy Adams; Norman and Muriel Davison, Hook; Stuart and Susan Vaughan; Tim Everson and staff of Kingston Heritage Centre; Neil White, Elmbridge Museum; Derek Jebbitt; David and Lorraine Evans; Roger Swan and Dave Swan; Arthur's Club, Dorking; Tim Howe; Paul Garett; Peter Forsdick, Hook; Graham Page; Panther Public House staff, Reigate; Ron Shettle; Ian Wakeford; Peter Ashley; Kathleen Bowyer; St Paul's Church, Hook, members; Gordon Wellard, Camberley. Surrey Heath Museum; Amanda Devonshire and staff of Runnymede Museum; Croydon Central Library; Mary Bryant, Paul Spence, Mrs E. Bates; Stuart Andrews; Paul Rutterford; Steve Kemp; Steve Clarke of Archive Records, Chertsey; Brian and Sally of Little Bookham Street; Gwen and Gary Poore; Christine and Neil McGinn; Marnie Wilson; John Stuart; Clive Ruby, Wallington; Alf De Araujo; Kennedy Memorial Trust; Alan Greenwood, Chobham; S. Hawkins, Kevin Gillen, Purley Library.

Photograph Credits

Dorking Museum (Dorking shops; Tiroler cafe and road protest); Greta Morley (Dorking traffic scenes); Ron Poore's family (Epsom clock tower, Sutton Phoenix Garage, Bletchingley street scenes); Bourne Hall Museum (Epsom street scenes); Surrey Local Studies Library (Guildford town scenes); Brian Bailey (Shanty Cafe, Weybridge); Ian Wakeford collection (Woking street scenes and shops); Brian Woodriff (Kingston trolleybus scenes except for the last day of running photographs – Espresso sign, Kingston); Elmbridge museum (Walton and Weybridge – Esher – Cobham scenes); Derek Jebbitt (Kingston's last day of trolleybuses, plus Surbiton and Hampton Court trolleybuses); Graham Page (Chessington Youth Club member and scenes – Tolworth Tower – Fine Fare and Tolworth Odeon – Georgie Fame and Jethro Tull performances) Kingston Heritage Centre (additional Kingston street scenes, Hook Underpass, New Malden village; Ron Shettle collection (Ripley fire); Garett family (solo picture of Paul Garett, the king mod); Epsom Herald archives (non-street scenes of Epsom; jockeys etc); Jack Underwood collection (Headline Girls); Jack Sales (Redhill High Street); Doris Murray and family (South Norwood wedding) Peter Ashley, Meadvale (Tatsfield in snow); Sutton Local Studies Library (Sutton street scenes); John Stuart (Jimmy Tarbuck at Sutton Granada); Roland Jonas, through Ron Head's archives (Godalming flood pictures); Richard Cooper collection (Horley carnival); Roger Swan and friends (Kingston Lambretta Club and skiffle band); Len's of Sutton (Twickenham trolley bus); Hazel Jackson (Lower Kingswood snowbound cars); Francis Studios Frimley (Frimley parade scene); Runnymede Museum at Chertsey (Chertsey assorted shop scenes – frozen Thames); Croydon Central Library (Croydon street scenes); David Tippett-Wilson of Hook (Hook Road, Hook Parade, Hook sign); Mrs Vaughan-Lewis, Surrey Records Office); Phillip Michael Didier; Surrey Local Studies (Guildford flood); Laurie James (GS bus to Ewhurst); Popperfoto (George Harrison's wedding photographs); Malcolm Pendrill (Reigate street scenes and back cover of Reigate High Street); Roy Quiddington (Redhill Colman's Institute); R. Shettle collection (Polesden Lacey fire); Les Kirkin of New Malden (various in Kingston borough).

Special thanks: *to Graham Page and Ian Wakeford for access to their fabulous photographic collections; Sonia Babister for allowing the pages of her 1964 diary to be opened; A.G. Cook for Horley contributions; Joan Mulcaster for Sutton information; Adam Forde for notes on Haslemere; Steve Kemp for extensive data on Chertsey's night life; the editors and staff of all the county's local weekly newspapers who have chronicled Surrey life so thoroughly; museum and library staff across Surrey who have preserved archives for all to enjoy and peruse, and press photographers who are with us no more but whose material has been saved from the skip by colleagues and their immediate families and friends.*

Front cover design: Mark Davison, Sean George.

Back cover: Reigate High Street in 1963. Photograph by Malcolm Pendrill FBIPP, FRPS, FRSA.

Logo: Cathie Shuttleworth.

Bibliography

Surrey Pubs by Richard Keeble (Batsford 1965); London's Telephone Exchanges (1927-1966); Stone Alone by Bill Wyman with Ray Coleman (Penguin); The Lives of John Lennon by Albert Goldman (Bantam); The Beatles – The Ultimate Recording Guide by Allen J. Wiener (Aurum Press); Genesis – a biography by Dave Bowler and Bryan Dray (Sidgwick and Jackson); The A-Z of the 1960s by Ann and Ian Morrison (Breedon); The Tillingbourne Bus Story by George Burnett and Laurie James (Middleton Press); The Amber Valley Gazeteer of Greater London's Suburban Cinemas 1946-86 by Malcolm Webb; The Surrey Weather Book (Frosted Earth); The Marc Bolan Story by Mark Paytress (Sidgwick and Jackson); Croydon the Story of a Hundred Years (Croydon Natural History and Scientific Society); British Hit Singles (Guinness); Top 40 Charts (Guinness); The Story of Camberley by Gordon Wellard; Ronald Biggs Odd Man Out (Bloomsbury 1994); The Surrey Comet series of newspapers; Surrey Mirror Series; Surrey Advertiser and News and Mail series; Sutton Herald, Epsom Herald, Dorking and Leatherhead Advertisers, Farnham Herald group and their associated titles; Croydon Advertiser and Richmond & Twickenham Times.

Rivalry at the coffee bars

Dorking and Leatherhead gangs clash at café

DORKING's young people of the Sixties had several favourite meeting places. One of them was The Tiroler coffee house in North Street which in later years became a building society. This venue was described as "very dark; a place where the young people gathered."

The Tiroler had a barman called Don, "a tall bloke who took no nonsense." He would serve Pepsi drinks with lemon, ice cubes and a straw. A Rockola juke box played five records for a shilling (5p).

Sometimes gangs would clash there and great rivalry existed between the lads of Leatherhead and the boys of Dorking. One resident recalled that they were always fighting because of the animosity between the two towns.

Dorking's young men cursed visits by Curly Bill and the Horsham boys who "were ferocious" and on one occasion nearly upturned an Austin 7 opposite the cafe.

A milk bar drew thirsty teenagers to the High Pavement in the High Street by the White Horse. It had tall stools with chrome bars on which sat girls in mini skirts "hoping to be noticed". The milk bar also sold Butler's mineral waters.

Also on High Pavement was Dipples, a retail shop specialising in exotic American cigarettes – Texas and Camel being favourites.

Teas and luncheons were on offer at The Rustic next to the Oddfellows Halls and it was here that a Mrs Bowden worked. Her husband, Merv, was to win the pools. In the early 1990s, this premises became a much-cherished music bar run until August 1994 by David and Lorraine Evans. Some of the singles played by DJs recalled the dizzy days of bygone Dorking.

The Deepdene cafe was kept by a John Smith who used to present rock and roll concerts at Dorking Halls and Epsom Baths. Coffee was also served in the Melody Barn at the back of a record shop in West Street which now forms part of an antiques arcade.

The mods used to buy their suits from Arthur Dipple at his tailors in the Rotunda at the foot of

The Tiroler café in North Street, Dorking, where teenagers gathered to listen to hit parade singles on a juke box. But sometimes youths from Leatherhead caused trouble.

Butter Hill in South Street. His youngest son, Mick, recalled many years later: "After the Teds, there were the Italian styles with short jackets and winkle-pickers and the sharp styles of the mods. They all got their suits from him."

Cliff Richard was just one of the big names who performed at the Dorking Halls in the 1960s. Another popular attraction was the Ted Heath Orchestra, some of whose members lived locally for years.

Some Dorking music-lovers recall Cliff Richard wearing a pink jacket, black and white shirt, black, slip-on shoes and white 'slacks' when he appeared at the Dorking Halls. The John Barry Seven, Chris Barber and Joe Brown were also said to be major attractions in their time.

The Halls also attracted crowds to see Billy Two Rivers in wrestling matches. Journalist Chris Porter, from the *Dorking Advertiser*, recalled: "He used to do a war dance when he got in a rage."

Protestors angry about plans to build a roundabout at the top of Wathen Road, Dorking, for a possible town by-pass, stage a demonstration in the street. On top of one of the cars is a board declaring: 'Let's save Dorking'.

Dorking, Brockham, Westcott, Shere, Abinger

'Let's save Dorking' protest

DORKING faced a crisis in the Sixties – where to put all the traffic as more and more families saved up to buy cars.

The old-style country town at the foot of the rolling downs was becoming increasingly congested with cars and lorries travelling on the A25 between Reigate and Guildford. The town lay right in the path of the east-west traffic and there was no real alternative route.

Matters came to a head when the 1963 town plan showed proposals for either a bypass or an inner relief road. The bypass would have carved through beautiful pastureland between Brockham and Shere. The relief road would have sliced through the recreation ground by the Mill Pond and protestors claimed it would have been a 64-feet wide dual carriageway "with metal barriers from end to end." The objectors feared the demolition of some 70 homes, and the local authorities seemed to have little concern about this, saying that most of the homes were built before 1900 and would

therefore not have much of a life left! The campaigners argued the town would have been cut in two.

There were angry demonstrations in the street and the picture (above) shows placard-waving protestors gathered at the top of Wathen Road, Dorking, where a roundabout would have been constructed, along with one at Star Corner in West Street. Residents eventually put great pressure on the Government to build a London orbital motorway to the north of Dorking and the M25 was mooted. In later decades this was to take a considerable amount of the east-west traffic and plans for alternative schemes were dropped in the late 70s. Its opening in the mid Eighties meant traffic through the villages was much eased. At Abinger Hammer, a decorator was able to pitch his ladder in the road without too much inconvenience for the first time in years.

In 1964 extensive widening work occurred on the A24 north of Dorking involving the demolition of some properties.

Waitrose led the way in self-service shopping in Dorking. This was how its store in South Street looked in 1967. In the window, posters advertise chicken at 2s 6d (12p) a pound, melons at 2s 3d (11p) each and Typhoo tea at 1s 4½d (7p) a quarter. When it opened, one housewife commented: "It was vast, cold and scared the life out of you." A Morris Traveller driver finds no difficulty in parking outside.

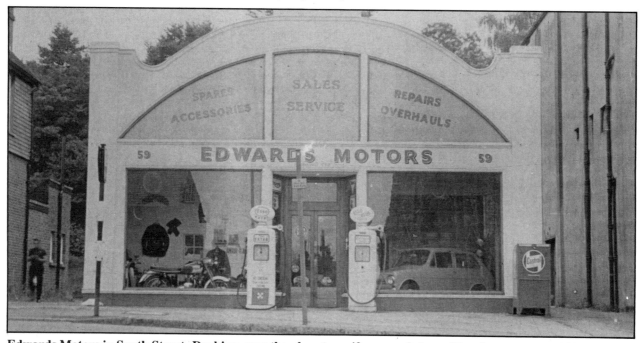

Edwards Motors in South Street, Dorking, was the place to go if you needed anything for your motorbike. It stood next to the Pavilion Cinema, which until its closure in September 1963, had served the town's cinema-goers since 1925. Edwards Motors was run as a family business and had passed through generations of the Edwards family. The two pumps outside offered Esso Extra and Esso Blue which an attendant would deliver to motorists pulling up in the road outside. At the rear, mechanics toiled away in workshops, repairing motorbikes and cars for customers. In more recent times, a DIY firm traded at the site.

The Pavilion pictured in September 1963 weeks after it closed for good.

"Only shutting for the summer"

Closure of Dorking's Pavilion

THE Pavilion Cinema in South Street, Dorking, closed "for the summer" in June 1963, never to re-open. It later became a DIY store but the building survived the bulldozer.

The last film to be shown at The Pavilion was a colour spectacular: Steve Reeves in Duel of the Titans. Cinema-goers referred affectionately to the picture house as "the flea pit" and talked of the "whole of the upstairs shaking" when watching films.

Dorking's remaining cinema was The Embassy, opposite Dorking Halls, which was closed in 1973 when it became a meeting place for Jehovah's Witnesses until its demolition in 1983. The Embassy had a restaurant above where young folk would while away a Saturday. Next to this cinema, work started in 1963 on Dorking's new telephone exchange, which was planned to be completed for a changeover to Subscriber Trunk Dialling (STD) in 1965-66.

The Pavilion later became Strawberry Studios. Rock group 10CC formerly Hot Legs – were in 1977 to record there and their album, Deceptive Bends was named after the sign warning of the sharp twists on the A24 at Mickleham Bends. Cliff Richard also recorded at the studios. In the 1980s, two-bed flats were rented above the ground floor which was used as Coombes' builders merchants.

The last advert to appear in the *Dorking Advertiser* for the Pavilion Cinema. It appeared in the Whitsun edition, 1963 and the following week, Shipman and King Cinemas (S and K) announced that the Pavilion would be closed "from June 10th until August 5th". It did not re-open.

No waiting this side today. There was parking on alternate days of the week in Dorking High Street in the mid Sixties as this picture shows. But two cyclists have taken no notice of the prohibition. The instruction on the sign could be changed according to which day of the week it was. On the left is the Wheatsheaf pub once kept by a publican named Moore; 'a big fellow with grey hair', according to ex patrons. At one time there was a bread oven at the back and meat was reported to have hung in a large cellar in the underground caves. The pub was closed by Allied Breweries on 20th January 1974 and its demise was described as "a great tragedy" by Mr Cyril Seman, then the planning officer for Dorking Urban Council. Townsfolk remember it as an "olde worlde" establishment. A quarter of a century on from its closure, the sign on the bar door glass could be still seen in a discount bookshop which occupied the premises.

The early 1960s outside the Wheatsheaf, Dorking High Street. The double decker may have been an RT 414 which ran between Horsham and West Croydon every hour or between Capel and West Croydon every 30 minutes.

Traffic in Dorking High Street outside A.R. Miller's cakes and bread shop opposite the White Horse.

Sixties' architecture vandalised the views

'Ugly' developments in Dorking

THE bland architecture of the 60s scarred Dorking's scenery. Federated House, an office block near Deepdene Station was permitted only after an appeal to central Government. The book, Dorking, a Surrey Market Town through 20 centuries, published by Dorking Local History Group, commented on the style of Federated House. "This grim, flat-roofed building of 1965 intruded most unhappily into all the distant views of the Mole Gap from Deepdene, Denbies, the Glory, Cotmandene, Box Hill or Pixham, offering testimony that planners of the period paid no regard to sight lines."

The same book comments that the Sixties' architecture was "often dreary; frequently ugly" and that "councillors were only too ready to allow historic buildings to be demolished rather than be restored."

In 1960-1, "visual damage" said the book, "was caused in South Street by the insertion of a series of starkly plain retail and office buildings into the homely 18th and 19th century frontages of both sides of the road near the Spotted Dog.

The High Street saw the Red Lion "regrettably" demolished in 1964 after its closure in 1959. It had been the haunt of many young folk in its time and its dimly lit cellar bar, The Shades, was a place to escape from the outside world. It was replaced by a "characterless block of five shops with flats above." It stood opposite where Etams and Lanes Bistro later traded.

Dorking High Street in the early Sixties, with Timothy Whites, Tylers confectioners, Collett's dress shop and Yates opticians. Other familiar sights, now disappeared, include Burton's, the outfitters and the sign to the Ministry of Labour. In the picture are cars which were commonplace at the time – a Ford 105E, MG Magnet and Hillman Minx, plus a Ford Anglia which first came off the new production plant at Halewood in Merseyside in 1962. The 425 bus from Dorking North Station ran two services: one to Guildford and the other a 'swinger' which turned round at the Cricketers public house, Westcott. In 1967, the 425 ran every half hour to Guildford, the morning rush hour service scheduled to take 55 minutes. There was even an hourly Sunday service on the 'well-trodden' route through Westcott, Wooton, Abinger, Gomshall and Shere to Guildford Bus Station in Farnham Road.

A 425 'RF' style bus for Westcott calling at the White Horse, Dorking, in the 1960s. Over the road are the stores, F.W. Woolworth's, Richard Hicks, the greengrocer's, later absorbed by Woolworth's and Pearks, a small grocery shop. Pearks "had cupboards all round with a worktop on which were piled packages and tins right up to the ceiling", according to one reminiscing resident. "It was run by a husband and wife team and it was always inundated with people." She added: "Really, it was quite claustrophobic in there with long queues." Another shopper could clearly remember the black and white tiled floor and the narrow passages.

ROVER 1963 a new swift and silent range

* The new sleek and stylish 3-Litre Coupé
* The Mark II 3-Litre saloon: swifter version of an elegant car
* The 110—faster, more powerful replacement for the 100
* The 95—luxury six-cylinder motoring for the family

Come and see these swift and silent Rover cars here. We shall be glad to arrange a demonstration run in any of them.

ROVER—ONE OF THE WORLD'S BEST ENGINEERED CARS

DORKING MOTOR CO (1958) LTD

REIGATE ROAD, DORKING   Tel. DORKING 4521/5

'Sleek and stylish' Rovers advertised in the Dorking and Leatherhead Advertiser during the late spring of 1963.

The Playhouse, Guildford, which stood in the High Street before the Tunsgate Arcade was built.

Women queue in cold for a ten shilling skirt

Guildford in 1963

IN January 1963, it was announced that £110,000 had been raised for the opening of the Yvonne Arnaud Theatre, expected in the summer of 1964.

People wishing to escape from the coldest winter since 1740 could book a holiday through Pickford's Travel in Onslow Street (Tel: Guildford 2997), where a week-long break to Paris was 11½ gns or a 15-day visit to the Costa Del Brava, 34½ gns.

If the water did not freeze, it was worth a visit to the new 'do-it-yourself' car wash at the Woodbridge Service Station. One clean in the 'automatic wash bay' was half a crown (12p).

The long icy spell meant many football matches around the county were postponed for weeks. At Guildford, despite the cancellations, there was at least outdoor training instead while a thaw was awaited.

Undeterred by the Arctic weather, 24 women queued in the cold for the January sale at Harvey's of Guildford. One lady had her eye on a 10s (50p) skirt. Meanwhile, hundreds of bargains were promised at the 'Remnant Day' in Gammons – 'the easy-walk-round store'.

Guildford Odeon offered some shelter from the elements and a visit in early January would have offered patrons Norman Wisdom in On The Beat. Alternatively, the Playhouse in the High Street was showing Jackie Gleason in Gigot.

Guildford Library's lending department in 1964 with its leatherette chairs. A caged budgerigar on top of the card files used to be an unusual attraction in the library. Rumour has it that the bird used to be able to recite certain lines of Shakespeare.

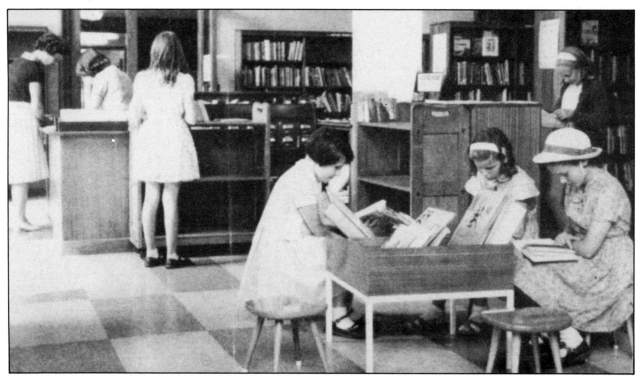

A corner of the children's library "in Guildford's handsome public library" opened in North Street, Guildford, in 1962.

Youths on scooters pull up at the new-look Sainsbury's supermarket in Guildford High Street in 1965.

Apart from the freezing weather in **January 1963**, other stories of the day included an outbreak of swine fever at Home Farm, Albury, and the fight by market traders in North Street, Guildford to stay on their present site rather than be moved to a development at Friary Square.

Indoors at the Civic Hall, out of the bitter winds, Chris Barber's jazz band helped people forget about the weather, while at Guildford Theatre, the chilling Agatha Christie play Spider's Web was performed. Meanwhile, at the Astoria cinema in Guildford, Pat Boone and Nancy Kwan starred in·The Main Attraction.

Frozen lavatories at Merrow School angered parents as the big freeze showed no signs of relenting. The new Hillman Minx, if purchased for £510 plus purchase tax (PA) of £106 16s 3d from Gray and Co Ltd of Woodbridge Meadows would have gone some way to beat the icy roads which prohibited some of the older cars from venturing out.

The inclement weather sometimes played havoc with the electricity supplies and the fluctuations interfered with television pictures in the area. Warm-hearted staff of the Central Electricity Generating Board helped alleviate the gloom by arranging for their staff's children to watch a show of Harry Corbett's Sooty and Sweep in Guildford.

Holiday companies took advantage of the cold weather misery to advertise breaks away from it all. *Surrey Advertiser* readers were enticed to Butlin's at Clacton, Margate, Bognor and Brighton for weekend holidays costing just £4.

Development work in Guildford was getting underway and a 'multi-tiered' car park and 15-storey office block were planned next to Guildford Station. There was bad news for 31 staff of Billing and Sons Ltd, printers and bookbinders of Guildford who were handed their notice.

Some villagers and townsfolk made the most of the freeze-up by devising a new winter sport – skating cars at Shalford Meadows. ". . . Then with headlights blazing, they accelerated, jammed on brakes and skidded in circles five to six times." Their antics, however, infuriated local ice skaters. Frozen pipes at a house in Bench Road, Guildford, were foolishly thawed out with a blow lamp: the heating was too much, and a fire broke out which severely damaged the large, snow-covered house.

Buryfields Clinic at Guildford.

Candlewick bedspreads for just 19/11 (slightly sub standard)

Also in January 1963, a furore broke out among Surrey's education chiefs after it was suggested that books and comics be put on desks of pupils sitting their 11 plus exams who may have finished papers early. "They would not last a minute before reading them," answered one critic.

By the third week of icy January, coal stocks were 'virtually exhausted'. A special train load of coal was sent to Guildford "but it was a drop in the ocean", the Coal Merchants Association told the *Surrey Advertiser*.

In **January 1963** King Bros in High Street, Guildford, offered Candlewick bedspreads for just 19s 11d (99p) – that is, the ones that were 'slightly sub standard'. Rhoyvl quilts were reduced to 57s 6d (£2.87) and flannelette cot sheets to 4s 11½d (25p).

Every Saturday, a disc jive was held at the Plaza in Guildford, while the Rotary Clubs planned 'premier balls' at Guildford Civic Hall to raise cash for the Yvonne Arnaud Theatre fund.

The Woodbridge Co-operative Society Supermarket lured housewives with:

Daz at 2s 6d (12½p)
Tide at 2s 6d (12½p)
Omo at 2s 6d (12½p)
Surf at 2s 6d (12½p)
– a saving of 3d a packet

On Wednesday, 23rd January 1963, the Mayor of Guildford, Alderman G.O. Swayne, formally inaugurated Guildford's 'magnificent new Civic Hall' – part of which had been in use for three months. The *Surrey Advertiser* reported the event as a 'glittering occasion'.

In **February 1963**, it was announced that plans had been drawn up for a new cattle market at Slyfield, Guildford. Meanwhile, Boots the chemist acquired the former premises of Marks and Spencer at 81-89 High Street, Guildford.

Later in the month, 12 traffic wardens were appointed to patrol central Guildford as a huge no-parking and limited waiting scheme was drawn up.

Villagers at Shalford suffered a blow when a fire severely damaged Shalford Church Hall in mid March.

A major plan to build a university at Guildford was unveiled in **March 1963**, which materialised in 1965 on a site near the Cathedral but there was an unholy row at Guildford Parish Church when the vicar, Reverend M.C. Brown, caused the choir to go on strike over a disagreement concerning harmony singing.

The Angel of Guildford was unveiled at the Cathedral after being surrounded by scaffolding for a considerable period; the work being hampered by the atrocious weather.

Firemen called to a chimney fire at the Royal Grammar School, Guildford, discovered a serious roof fire which swept through the top part of the ancient and renowned building. The blaze occurred in 1962. The car on the left is a fire officer's vehicle.

Fires sweep theatre, Grammar School; huge CND gathering at Cathedral

Ban The Bomb rally in Guildford

DURING **April 1963**, a serious fire occurred at Guildford Theatre. In the early hours of Wednesday 10th April, the stage and auditorium were completely destroyed by fire.

People were awoken by a huge explosion at dawn which rocked the town. By the time the Fire Brigade arrived, the theatre roof was blazing from end to end. And the roof of the rear portion of the Co-op premises had also fallen in. Firemen had to rescue people from the windows of the Haydon Place flats above the shops nearby in North Street. The theatre in earlier times was the Guildford Borough Hall and in 1924 was the courtroom where the prisoner, Jean-Pierre Vaquier was sentenced to death for murdering Alfred Jones, landlord of the Blue Anchor, Byfleet.

Two thousand people marched to Guildford Cathedral from all directions 'in jeans, sweaters, donkey jackets, wind cheaters, top hats, bowlers and cowboy hats' in a massive CND Ban The Bomb rally. Some even brought along transistor radios, record players, guitars and bugles. A number of girls 'danced to the Locomotion from one of the record players'.

With the disappearance of the snow and the appearance of spring sunshine, it was time to think about cameras, and Guildford's Timothy Whites offered Brownie 127s for 25s (£1.25). It was also the season to start mowing the grass. Viceroy side-wheel lawnmowers were available at the same store for 76s (£3.80) and a grass box would be added for 11s 6d (57p).

In **June 1963**, a new £100,000 river bridge was planned at Woodbridge, Guildford.

Lord Nugent visits the Slyfield Green Industrial Training Centre at Guildford and talks to an apprentice in June 1969.

The new Guildford Youth Centre's 'fully equipped' canteen in February 1966.

Guildford's new youth centre

THE new Guildford Youth Centre was fully running by February 1966, and the picture above shows some of its first customers being served at the canteen by the Guildford Youth Officer, Mr E. W. Tait.

The group in the photograph are a party of senior university students from New Zealand who were visiting Britain for a month as the guests of the Commonwealth Relations Office. They toured the new youth centre in Leapale Road, Guildford, and stopped for refreshments. On the shelves of the canteen were a variety of sweets and chocolates including Munchies, Bounties and McVities digestives to accompany a coffee at 9d (4p) a mug. Hot soup was also available at 1s (5p) a cup. Don't forget to return empty cups to the bar!

Guildford Youth Centre's smart new premises in Leapale Road in January 1967.

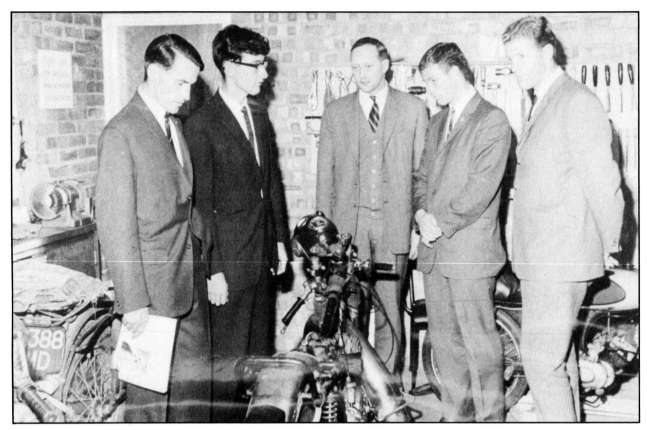

Youth workers from New Zealand examine the motorbike workshops at the new Guildford Youth Centre in February 1966. Third from left is Guildford Youth Officer Mr E.W. Tait. On the wall, a notice states: Please use the goggles which are provided for your own safety.

ODEON THEATRE GUILDFORD
Telephone 4770

MONDAY, MARCH 18th :: 6.0 & 8.15

LARRY PARNES presents

★ "YOUR LUCKY STARS" ★

starring

JOE BROWN

THE TORNADOS

SUSAN MAUGHAN, JESS CONRAD, EDEN KANE, ROLF HARRIS, SHANE FENTON, PETER JAY & THE JAYWALKERS, AL PAIGE

SEATS at : 10/6, 8/6, 5/6

Top stars of 1963 were appearing at the Guildford Odeon in March. Fenton became Alvin Stardust.

The coffee bar at Guildford Youth Centre c.1966

Traffic on the A3 at Ladymead, Guildford, in 1969.

Careful not to wobble! London Road, Guildford, in 1969.

The end of Woodbridge Road, Guildford, crossing North Street, with Swan Lane opposite. This view shows a typical 1969 traffic scene.

Stoke Road, junction of Park Road, Guildford, in the late Sixties.

The traffic direction sign to Charterhouse which was in place in the 1960s at Farncombe and which guided motorists for at least three more decades from the same spot.

Housemaster broke up concert — there was nearly a riot

Charterhouse boys formed top rock group Genesis

GENESIS, one of rock music's biggest acts of all time began its early life at Charterhouse School in Godalming.

The band was formed in 1968 from members of two other acts, The Garden Wall and Anon. Both these young groups comprised pupils of the fee-paying boarding school which was well-known for its repressive Victorian discipline.

Frowned upon by masters at the public school, the creative talents of Peter Gabriel, Tony Banks,

Mike Rutherford and Anthony Phillips could not be suppressed.

Social revolution was the issue of the day. The Beatles and Rolling Stones epitomised this. There was the rise of flower power, vigorous student unrest on the Continent and protests against the United States' involvement in Vietnam. In addition, there was a quickly-expanding drug culture. All these dramatic events were reflected in the music of the day.

With all this going on in the outside world, it was no wonder that young musicians trapped in the

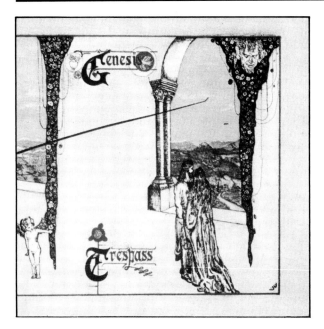

Trespass, the album by Genesis which was penned in a cottage at Dorking.

confines of a public school such as Charterhouse, should express themselves powerfully through their music.

"They say you can tell an ex-public schoolboy in prison because he takes to it like a duck to water," Peter Gabriel told Options magazine in 1987.

Not keen on sport, Rutherford, Gabriel and Phillips spent all their time writing and playing their music. Peter Gabriel arrived at the school in 1963 at the age of 13. The 1959 top three record by Johnny and the Hurricanes, Red River Rock, is one of the first recordings to awaken his love of rock music.

One of the few cherished freedoms enjoyed by the boys was the opportunity to play the piano in the dining hall. There was always a rush to get there first after classes. Peter Gabriel often tried to arrive first by climbing through serving hatches, according to the book, 'Genesis', by Dave Bowler and Bryan Dray (published by Sidgwick and Jackson Ltd.).

Tony Banks's prized possession was his drum kit and at 15, he played briefly with an r and b outfit, The Spoken Word. Mike Rutherford, from Cheshire, entered the school in 1964, being slightly younger than Banks and Gabriel. He had been playing the guitar since the age of seven. He later said of Charterhouse: "Without playing and writing, I'd have gone crazy." He became friends with Anthony Phillips, who joined the school in April 1965 at the age of 13 and they played music together.

Mike Rutherford later joined the group, Anon, in which guitarist Phillips was actively involved. Meanwhile Banks and Gabriel had formed Garden Wall.

Another musical pupil, Richard McPhail from Anon decided to mark his departure from Charterhouse in the summer of 1966 by putting on a concert intended to emanate the atmosphere of the Marquee in London where he went to see bands play. Some of the stick-in-the-mud staff were aghast at the idea of a rock concert at Charterhouse, and the book quotes a source as saying, "They just saw pop music as the revolution that was going to bring everything down."

The show was eventually allowed, providing no public announcements were made from the stage and it was held in broad daylight in the school hall and right at the end of term, presumably so that no student unrest could be sustained. The gig included songs such as When A Man Loves A Woman, the number two 1966 hit by Percy Sledge, and the Miracles' Motown classic You Really Got A Hold On Me. Gabriel dressed very rebelliously in a kaftan and beads and threw rose petals into the air.

The Garden Wall set was followed by Anon's, during which a song announcement was made. This prompted a music master to storm the stage in a rage and shout, 'No announcements!' He stopped the show at which there was 'nearly a riot'.

In the Easter holidays of 1967, Banks, Rutherford, Gabriel and Phillips entered a recording studio for the first time and in the next couple of years enlisted the help of another former Charterhouse pupil, Jonathan King, who, in 1965 had been in the top five with Everyone's Gone To The Moon, and had since turned to musical production.

Their early singles on Decca failed to make any impression but despite musical differences, King persuaded them to record an album, From Genesis To Revelation. The album could not bear the name Genesis because there was a band in America with the same title. One single, The Silent Sun, was frequently played on Radio Caroline before the ship had to flee the English seas. Chris Stewart, who was still at Charterhouse as a pupil, decided to quit Genesis but the others went from strength to strength. In November 1969, they lived together in a National Trust property near Dorking where they composed the much-acclaimed album, Trespass. They stayed at the cottage until April 1970, using a bread van to convey their equipment. Here, in the Surrey countryside, they were able to work undistracted on their talented compositions and form a foundation on which to build their astonishing careers.

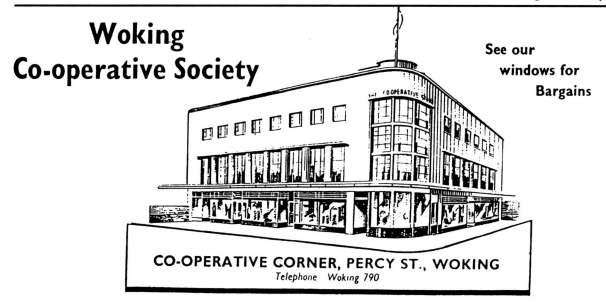

Woking Co-operative Society

See our windows for Bargains

CO-OPERATIVE CORNER, PERCY ST., WOKING
Telephone Woking 790

Woking, Byfleet, Weybridge, West End, Bisley, Horsell, Pirbright

Woking in the early Sixties

HERE is a digest of the news during the first quarter of the Sixties in the Woking, Byfleet, Knaphill and Sheerwater area as reported at the time.

January 1960: Woking's infamous landmark, the Stepbridge, which has dominated the stage for almost a quarter of a century, no longer exists. The stark, treacherous, but familiar framework, which stood bleakly over the Basingstoke Canal, was demolished completely on Wednesday 6th January.

Work is going on apace on the new Byfleet Loop Road which will save through traffic negotiating the tortuously winding High Road. On Saturday 9th January, the road was opened by Rt Hon. Harold Watkinson, Minister of Defence and MP for Woking.

Women with their hair in curlers dashed into the street on 11th January when fire broke out following an explosion at Michael Andrew's Hair Fashion Salon in Walton Road, Woking.

February 1960: The tallest chimney in the town, that of the former Woking Power Station is coming down, piece by piece. The chimney had been visible as far away as Merrow and the Chobham Ridges.

A one-way system drawn up for Woking's Commercial Road, Chertsey Road, Broadway and Duke Street.

It is announced that the Army's Inkerman Barracks at St John's, the depot of the Royal Military Police are to be sold. The Redcaps had occupied the site since moving from Mytchett in 1947.

His Royal Highness, the Duke of Edinburgh, visited the Welsh Guards at Pirbright Camp on St David's Day, Tuesday 1st March. He arrived by helicopter from Buckingham Palace in bright sunshine.

In test flights of the Vanguard aeroplanes, made by Vickers of Weybridge, hundreds of staff enjoyed free trips to European and Mediterranean cities. The Vickers Vanguard is the world's only second generation propellor-jet passenger plane.

March 1960: One of Woking's worst traffic accident blackspots – the junction of St John's Road with St John's Hill, has been improved beyond recognition.

Severe fire destroys roof of 14-bedroomed Manor Croft in The Ridgeway, Horsell.

April 1960: Four hundred and fifty Guards from the Guards Depot at Caterham marched into their new home in Pirbright Camp. Caterham had been their base for 83 years.

New head post office opens on 6th April at Commercial Road, Woking.

Two thousand five hundred workers on strike at Vickers, Weybridge, over dismissal of six men who

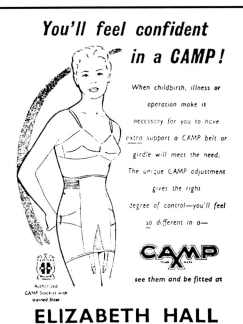
Getting the support you need in 1960.

refused transfer from working on Vickers' Vanguard to a VC10.

Work underway on the new Catholic Church at Sheerwater.

Major fire on 20th April at Crater Products, Lower Guildford Road, Knaphill.

May 1960: Statue of General Charles George Gordon, the 'hero of Khartoum' re-erected at Gordon Boys School, West End. Unveiled on Saturday 14th May by Lady Huddleston, widow of the former Governor General of Sudan.

New Horsell swing-bridge opened over the Basingstoke Canal. Mr A. Benstead, senior member of Woking Council, performed the ceremony.

Woking Council on Tuesday, 24th May, elected their first ever woman chairman, Mrs Dorothy Evelyn Gale, a Conservative member for St John's since 1954.

June 1960: A coloured teacher from the Gambia, Samuel Suru Rendall, electrocuted himself in a classroom at West Byfleet County Secondary School after he was asked to resign over his affair with a woman teacher.

One hundred protestors led by a kilted Scot marched through Woking on Saturday 11th June

There was exciting news at the pumps in April 1960.

in protest at the supply of nuclear arms to West Germany.

Woking Council draws up plans for a multi-storey car park on the White Rose Grange site.

Vickers sells ten Super VC10 airlines to BOAC.

July 1960: The Queen paid a 90-minute visit to the National Rifle Association and the famous Bisley Ranges on Friday 15th July. The Queen wore a floral dress with a primrose coat and floral hat.

More than 300 acres of Wisley Common handed to the people of Surrey by County Council Chairman Sir Cyril Black.

August 1960: Miss Margaret Finch chosen as Miss Pirbright 1960 at Pirbright Youth Club fete on 6th August.

Furore over the dozens of cyclists who park their machines nose to tail along the kerbs of Woking town centre.

Six hundred sign petition to save Byfleet Fire Station.

Idea of a prison at Bisley Boys School site mooted. The school closed in the summer of 1960.

September 1960: Ban The Bomb slogans daubed on railway embankment wall in High Street, Woking.

The shopping centre at Knaphill near Woking in the mid Sixties. Taylor's sweet shop on the left of the zebra crossing advertises Cornettos at 1s (5p), while next door, a couple are window shopping at The Shoe Box. Over the road is the Co-op, and Bon Marche newsagents.

October 1960: Widespread floods after heavy rain but fortunately, no houses under water.

A family escaped injury when a motorcycle combination crashed in Church Hill, Ottershaw, while on an outing . . . "a very popular form of Sunday afternoon enjoyment."

King Mahendra of Nepal visits Vickers Armstrong, Weybridge, with his wife, Queen Ratna, on 20th October.

November 1960: Three hundred teenagers petitioned the Ritz, Woking, to fit double seats in the back rows of the 3s 3d section. Their request turned down because it's illegal to have double seats in places of entertainment.

December 1960: The Gaumont Cinema in Chertsey Road, Walton, is being demolished along with other buildings, including the Sunray restaurant for a new shopping parade.

January 1961: Concern over attack of girl in Heathfield Road, Woking – second such incident.

January sales at Scotts in Commercial Road included Nathan dining tables at 11 gns. and Myers' bunk beds at £29. 15s 0d, 'including matresses'.

A court was told of a fight at Kaye's coffee bar, Bath Road, Woking. A builder's labourer was 'gaoled' for four months after the fracas involving a group of teenagers.

Grays travel bureau offer air fares to Paris for £9 19s 0d.

Three new, one-man buses with centre doors tried out on the 427, 437 and 456 London Transport routes between Woking and Weybridge.

A stabbing incident at SPD, Sheerwater.

Drunkenness among young people in Woking increases as more and more go into pubs.

February 1961: Automatic refuse collectors introduced by council's dustmen.

Furore over Chobham Road parking ban. Lobbies to Government.

April 1961: High density developments planned by council near Guildford Road, Claremont Avenue, north of park to White Rose Lane. Outcry by townsfolk followed. (Minister of Housing later approved scheme in May 1962.)

Ten year old boy nearly died when he sank in a bog by the Basingstoke Canal, Chertsey Road. Dramatic rescue by two youths.

May 1961: John Linscott Goode appointed new headmaster of Woking Grammar School.

'10,000 miles a year for £26' but tragedy strikes . . .

Bubble cars in the news

An advertisement in the *Woking News and Mail* in April 1962 for the Trojan 200 bubble car.

Dangerous bikers at Cobham

The carefree attitude of some young roadusers often landed them in court.

In early January, 1963, two youths were each fined £5 each and disqualified from driving for 18 months for the way they tore through Cobham on their motorcycles.

While in the execution of his duty, Police Constable Eric Humphreys noticed two motorbikes hurtle down the Portsmouth Road with their riders "crouched over the handlebars" as they raced through a 30mph area at up to 50mph.

The two culprits, both from Tartar Road, Cobham, were also ordered to pay 10s 6d (52p) costs by Kingston magistrates after hearing that a motor car driver had to swerve and brake sharply when they nearly collided with him.

Y ADVERTISER AND COUNTY TIMES SATURDAY JANUA

BUBBLE CAR DRIVER DIED AFTER BEING CUT FREE

BAD road conditions were blamed by an inquest witness at Guildford on Thursday for a fatal crash between a bubble car and a Land Rover just outside the factory of Vokes Ltd. at Henley Park,

The *Surrey Advertiser* of 5th January 1963 reports on the bubble car tragedy at Normandy near Pirbright.

THE bubble car is synonymous with the early Sixties and when it was introduced in 1962, it became a popular vehicle for young folk to get about in.

Continental Motor Cycles of Chertsey Road, Woking, advertised the vehicle in the *Woking News and Mail* in April 1962 declaring it was one of the cheapest ways to get around. One complete fill-up costs little more than 17 shillings (85p) the advertisement stated. It said that if the car was to do 10,000 miles a year, the total bill for oil and petrol is not likely to exceed £26 – just 10 shillings (50p) per week. A new Trojan bubble car would have cost just under £350.

There was justifiable concern from some people that the lightweight vehicles would not come out of traffic accidents as well as some cars.

In one horrific accident on the Pirbright Road, Normandy, at the end of December 1962, a bubble car was involved in an accident with a Land Rover. The bubble car driver, a girl aged 25, from Farnham, was trapped in the wreckage and had to be cut free by firemen. She later died from her injuries. On the slushy roads following the icy weather, the bubble car was seen to wobble and slew out of control, an inquest at Guildford was later told.

In another crash elsewhere in Surrey, a driver involved in a collision told a magistrates court that a bubble car had reversed into him. He was told he could well be lying for the bubble car didn't have a reverse gear.

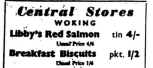

Woking News & M

No. 3443   FRIDAY, JUNE 16, 1961   T:

WINKLEPICKERS UNSUITABLE FOR CHILDREN...
– MEDICAL OFFICER

WHAT type of footwear does your son wear to go to school? In his report to the North-West Divisional Education Executive on Wednesday, Dr. C. A. McPherson, Divisional Medical Officer, had this to say: 'In the Secondary Schools some commendations have been forthcoming as to the neatness of the girls' hair styles, which compare more favourably with the footwear adopted by many of the senior boys.'

'Excessively pointed shoes, in general, are hardly to be regarded as suitable for adolescents of either sex, if only from a nuisance point of view, and it would be unfortunate if the future male generation was to be exposed to orthopaedic problems usually associated with those of the opposite sex,' said the doctor.

The report goes on to say that apart from the natural increase in the population of the Division, it had continued to be a priority area for housing development, and this was reflected by a further increase of just over 1,000 in the school population, which was subject to periodic medical inspection. This reached a total of 31,146 in 194 maintained primary and secondary schools, two residential nursery schools and two private schools.

The provision of additional and moveable classrooms at the schools to cope with the increased numbers tended to throw a strain on the available washing, lavatory, cloakroom and school meal facilities, unless these were correspondingly increased.

During the year school medical officers inspected maintained schools in their areas as to their hygienic condition. From these reports it was pleasing to see that some progress was being made in the provision of hot water facilities for hand washing, in providing new school kitchens and dining halls and in improving in others.

Container meals from central...

Society of Medical Officers of Health have addressed themselves to the problem of the sale of biscuits and sweets in school breaks. They pointed out that this was becoming increasingly common and was spreading into primary schools.

It was hoped that something might be done to discourage the spread and in the schools where it was already established that less objectionable foods, such as apples, nuts, raisins and potato crisps, might perhaps be sold instead.

WOKING SQUADRON HAS 'DONE WELL'

More Changes

After last three months' work, the improvements to the junction of Shores Road with Chobham Road, Woking, are nearing completion. The improvements include widening Shores Road to a 24ft. carriageway, construction of a 6ft footpath and ...tion of street lighting at the junction. Contractors are still working on the widening of the entire length of Shores Road and are expected to complete this task by the autumn. [Photo: D. Morum].

FETE: IMPORTANT EVENT

PREGNA...
TELLS...
FIFTEEN-YEAR-O...

Headlines from the Woking News and Mail of 16th June, 1961.

May 1961: "Misconceived monstrosities which are being erected in the very heart of the village" is how Mr A. Benstead described the development in Horsell. "I cannot imagine who could plan that such modern buildings of such height should overlook the churchyard whose peaceful serenity has been undisturbed for centuries," he said.

June 1961: Medical officers expressed concern that 'winklepickers worn by adolescents may lead to orthopaedic problems normally associated with the opposite sex in later years.'

July 1961: The first Saturday of the month saw temperatures hit a reported 95F (35C) and over 4,500 cooled off at Woking Swimming Pool. It had been the hottest day 'since 1954'.

Princess Marina opened Brookwood's Patients' Social Club and Centre.

August 1961: An elderly woman was bound and gagged by robbers in her home at Fowlers Well Farm, Chobham.

September 1961: Details of Woking Council's £140,000 civic centre plans unveiled.

October 1961: On 2nd October, The Midland Bank opened a branch at 13 High Street, Knaphill.

The new headmaster of Woking Boys Grammar School, Mr J.L. Goode, feared that the fashion of young males had undergone great changes in a few years and envisaged a chaotic situation if it is not checked. 'Shirts and socks should be of a quiet colour.'

Kenwood Manufacturing announced it had grown out of its Woking site and was moving with 700 redundancies possible.

November 1961: Ten-storey block of 34 flats planned at Craigmore, Guildford Road, Woking.

December 1961: Countess Adelina de Lara, the world famous pianist who had lived the last 30 years of her life in Woking, died at the end of the month.

Woking Community Centre opened on 26th November.

A mysterious abandoned Italian plane was impounded at Fairoaks Aerodrome, Chobham.

Some residents of Rydens Way, Old Woking, in the summer of 1965: Mrs Patricia Simmons with her children Lee and Crishna. The latter grew up to be head librarian at Woking Central Library.

A busy shopping day in Chertsey Road, Woking.

Commercial Road, Woking, with the Atalanta on the left.

Rolling Stones, Cream . . . and fights

Atalanta Ballroom, Woking

WOKING's Atalanta Ballroom was the place to be in the 1960s and many top rhythm and blues bands played there, including the Rolling Stones. The venue boasted the best sprung floor in Surrey.

Trendy teenagers told their parents they were "going up the 'Atta'" as it was known. A visitor in those days was Jackie Everett who later recalled: "It was a rough place. There were regular fights there."

Surrey dee-jay Steve Kemp remembered: "The discos always had trouble. When they played more of the soul and Motown music favoured by the mods, there were punch-ups."

On 19th August 1963, the Rolling Stones perfor-med at the Atalanta. Earlier that day, they had gathered to listen to a pressing of Poison Ivy which was due to be the follow-up single to Come On, which was that week number 24 in the charts. Come On later nudged its way up to 21 the following month. Poison Ivy was later withdrawn and replaced with I Wanna Be Your Man.

Bill Wyman later wrote that August 1963 was probably the most exciting month of any for the Stones and the teenagers of the day. The cult TV programme Ready Steady Go was launched on 9th August and the band were invited to play on its second ever show, on 26th August, after the produc-tion team spotted them playing to 800 people at the Richmond Athletic Ground on 18th August – the day before the Woking concert.

The Atalanta, Woking. This famous night spot had a hair stylist's on the first floor. Note the adverts for Coca Cola and razor blades. Bath Road is on the left.

Woking historian Ian Wakeford revealed a humorous anecdote about the Atalanta. "Many Woking men claim they first met their wives there, but you seldom come across a woman who confesses to have ever been there."

The ballroom was demolished in 1972 to make way for town centre redevelopment but the memories remain. Mothercare, Robert Dyas and Concept Care later stood on the site.

The pop scene was beginning to explode in Surrey in 1962, and dance halls in the Woking area, as in the whole of the country, were starting to rock, twist, jive and hop. These adverts from the *Woking News and Mail* from the spring of 1962 capture the mood.

It's 1962 and the dance halls come alive

Teens get jiving

Robinson's the drapers and department store in Chertsey Road in the Sixties, long before McDonald's burger restaurant took over the ground floor. Robinson's had four floors and a restaurant at the top reached by way of stairs or a lift. Customers would grab a tray and queue up for the self-service food before sitting down on the orange-coloured imitation leather seating. Orange was also the background colouring on the shop fascia outside which bore the shop's name. Note the reflection in the top windows of a crane working over the road. In earlier times, the post office was situated next door to the store. In the late Sixties, there was a fire in the restaurant which many townsfolk still remember.

Torn off a strip in Sainsbury's, Woking

High Street, Woking. On the right is Farnham Carpets, and two doors along, Sainsbury's, with its modern shop fascia, but old-fashioned counter service inside. One resident of Old Woking remembers as a six year old child, tearing his short trousers on the sharp edge of one of the counters and being told off by his mother. Between Sainsbury's and Farnham Carpets was Sam Cook, the fruiterer whose other branches included Victoria Road, Surbiton. To the right of Sainsbury's was de Neuville, hair stylists.

Chertsey Road, Woking, circa 1963. On the right hand side is Boots, outside which is parked a bubblecar. Next door was Freeman Hardy Willis, whose neighbours were Timothy White's and the Home and Colonial tea stores. And then came T.E. Russell, the jeweller, who closed in 1993. He was one of the last surviving individual traders in the town. Between 1964 and 1968 there was no change in the shops in this part of the parade. The Boots store in modern times was a Pizza Hut.

High Street, Woking, in the mid 1960s. On the left is Colman's furniture store, later to become Courts. Edwards, the draper's, is next door. This store later closed and became two units. In 1994, one was empty and the other was Mr Cod. An RF single decker bus approaches from the direction of Barclays Bank.

Rosemont Terrace, West Byfleet. The first shop on the right is Sainsbury's, then Eastman's, dyers and cleaners; Horstmanns opticians, followed by the Wine Cellars Ltd and MacFisheries. Further down was de Neuville ladies' hair stylists.

Drunkenness on the increase in Woking

Young Ones at the Ritz

AT the start of 1962, Adam Faith appeared in What A Whopper and Bob Hope in Bachelor In Paradise at the Ritz, Woking.

January 1962: Twenty five snowclearers used by Woking Council to clear the heavy fall of snow. Fifty tons of salt used. The depth of snow was up to eight inches – the greatest fall since 13th January 1955. In the physiotherapy department at Woking's Victoria Hospital, it was only 34F (1C) and there were many complaints.

Maxwell's Stores in Woking decided to close on Mondays and open all day Wednesdays so staff "like J.S. Sainsbury's" can have two consecutive days' holiday.

At the cinema, Elvis Presley appeared in Blue Hawaii and Cliff Richard in The Young Ones.

Drunkenness was up in Woking for the fourth successive year.

In **April 1962**, Princess Margaret and Lord Snowdon viewed Vickers' new airliner being prepared for a test flight when they made a visit on Wednesday 25th April. It was a gloriously sunny day for their trip. On 28th, Woking's new athletic ground was opened by Lt Col H.J. Wells, chairman. **May 1962**, saw four Liberals win seats on Woking Council – 'the first ever representation on the council.'

'Hop' sessions were held at Woodham village hall and there was 'swinging from 8 until 12' at Horsell village hall in **July 1962**, with a 'beach ball hop'.

One of the first office blocks to be built in Woking was Premier House, pictured here when Maples, the furniture store traded on the ground floor. In the background is the Co-op, in modern times replaced by Toys 'R' Us. This was the junction of the old Percy Street and Commercial Road which is now called Commercial Way.

Byfleet Green in the 60s. On the far right is Wasley's butcher's, and working along the street is the Midland Bank, Gas Showrooms and beyond these, the Plough Inn. Across the road is Binfield bakery.

High Road, Byfleet, at the junction with Church Road with the Blue Anchor in the foreground. The shop is Digby's, the grocer's.

The Green, Byfleet, also known as Plough Corner. On the right hand side of Oyster Lane is the Mid Surrey Motors garage and Horace Freeland and Co., ironmongers.

Firemen edge their way towards the inferno in Ripley in February 1969.

A very serious fire swept through Polesden Lacey in September 1960. Surrey Fire Brigade's newly acquired control unit can be seen on the right along with a divisional officer's car – the black model – which was equipped with an orange flashing warning light on the roof and an electric bell on the front bumper. The white car was probably the chief officer's.

Ripley High Street soon after the arrival of the Fire Brigade.

High Street a ball of flame

The great fire of Ripley, 1969

ONE of the most spectacular fires to occur in a Surrey village for many years put Ripley in the headlines in February 1969.

A tanker driver delivering paraffin to a hardware store realised to his horror that while filling the shop's tank, on the first floor, it was seriously overflowing and highly inflammable fuel was gushing through the ceiling into the shop premises below.

The driver immediately ran to his lorry to switch off the pump and on returning to the shop found it a mass of flames. Realising that staff were still inside, he ran around to the front of the premises and raised the alarm. Then he speedily returned to his lorry only to find that the delivery hose still connected to the tanker was on fire. He seized a knife and hurriedly hacked through the hose before driving the tanker to safety.

Gas cylinders stored at the shop, which belonged to Richard Green, then started to explode, and with a loud bang, the back wall of the store blew out. Debris flew in all directions. One piece of a gas cylinder travelled nearly 200 yards away to damage chimney pots, tiles, and a TV aerial on the roofs of distant houses.

A huge evacuation operation of nearby homes was carried out and traffic diverted off the A3 at Send. On the opposite side of what was then the A3, cars in a showroom were threatened by heat radiation and were moved. About two dozen houses suffered varying degrees of damage from heat or flying debris. It was sheer good fortune that the petrol storage tank under the shop's forecourt was not involved.

Forty brave firemen from Guildford, Woking, Esher and Camberley tackled the inferno while trying to ward off both the intense heat plus flying debris. Eventually, after much of the paraffin had been burned, the flames died down and the fire could be quelled. It was certainly one of historic Ripley's most memorable disasters.

A Ford Consul, Vauxhall Velox or Wyvern and Ford Anglia are parked with ease in Church Street, Walton, during the Sixties. Choice fruits and fresh vegetables are available from Langley's on the left, together with Lyons tea. Sun blinds are pulled down to shield the wares in A. Snell's, in the centre, while on the right is 'Walton's leading store', Birkheads, which stood almost opposite Ron's, where Pepsi Cola could be purchased on a hot summer's day.

A Wolseley 1500 and Vauxhall Cresta with a Hillman Minx in the background parked in Church Street, Walton, outside W.F. Birkhead and Son's, outside of which hangs flags advertising Bush and Murphy televisions. Next door, on the right is the Wool Shop.

A bicycle and a bubble car are the only wheels in motion in Church Street, Walton in this picture taken from the High Street junction. There was usually no reverse gear on bubble cars and parking in garages was not advised. The side-hinged door opened upwards and outwards.

Walton — Weybridge — Addlestone — Hersham

Bouffant hair-dos at Walton Playhouse

THE young people of Walton and Weybridge were really swinging in the Sixties and there was no better place to be than the Playhouse in Walton.

It was here that up and coming Weybridge pop band The Nashville Teens would pack out a Saturday night. Girls wearing short skirts, bouffant hair-dos, shoes, stockings or tights would have their hands stamped in the entrance hall before going in with boys in winklepickers to see the group that made top ten hits such as Tobacco Road and Google Eye in 1964.

Young folk used to come from Hersham, Addlestone, Chertsey and further afield to see their chart-busting heroes, but in order to control their excitement, there was no alcohol on sale — only cola. Some of the braver youngsters slipped out of the venue to visit local pubs before attempting re-admission to the sprung-floored ballroom.

The evenings went on from 8 o'clock until midnight but the last bus to Hersham was 11.35. Some would rather wait until closing time to hop on the station bus which ran only half way to Hersham.

The Shanty Cafe next to Weybridge Station provided refreshments for weary travellers. It was run by a foreign gentleman and appeared to be more like an American *sarsaparilla* bar. It used to have large plastic ice cream cones outside and served delicious milkshakes, including ones with a banana flavour. In modern times it traded as Buffers wine bar.

Not such a friendly rendezvous point was the High Spot, a dance hall and notorious trouble spot over the top of Burton's in Walton High Street. It was reached by way of stairs at the side of the shop, and up these climbed the rival gangs from Shepperton, Byfleet and Walton. They often fought each other and became involved in clashes with other groups who had come down from as far as Elephant and Castle in South London.

In the Beehive Cafe in Walton High Street, next door to Burton's, frothy espresso coffee was a favourite. Youths would sit around tables covered with gingham check cloths and smoke Woodbine cigarettes, usually on a Sunday afternoon before the Regal Cinema opened for the evening. The Regal was in New Zealand Avenue where decades later, Payless DIY centre stood. Dances were often held at Addlestone's Co-op Hall on a Sunday and many a couple held their wedding reception at the venue. It was demolished in 1993.

For the younger children of the district, ballet classes were held by Kathleen Grist in the Walton Working Men's Club in Church Road. Every year in the 60s she staged shows in the Walton Playhouse to raise money for research into cancer. She was a single lady who was a very petite blonde and she certainly knew her job. Kathleen Grist continued to live in the Walton area for the next three decades.

Residents fondly recall the 'unlikely' destinations of the Green Line buses, one of which was the 716 service from Addlestone to Stevenage. Many children had no idea where Stevenage was.

One of the biggest employers was the BAC Vickers works where some 4000 people toiled, and Hersham's Hackbridge engineering company which employed in the region of 1,200 people. The firm used to make the largest transformers in the world and when they moved equipment to and from the site, roads had to be closed for people's safety. The heavy loads were accompanied by police escorts.

Among the shops in Walton were Lipton's, International, Sainsbury's, Macfisheries and Woolworth's. The latter had three aisles down the shop and assistants standing behind each counter. The floor was formed from wooden blocks and near the entrance stood tall, red weighing scales.

Major work on Walton's modern shopping centre and flats took place during the decade and still bears the distinctive characteristics of those contemporary architects.

Sainsbury's in Weybridge High Street, like other branches in Surrey, had individual counters for the various foodstuffs until modernisation drastically changed these outlets to self-service. This picture was taken months after decimalisation arrived, shortly after the Sixties gave way to the Seventies. People vividly recall the butter being patted into shape, according to what weight was required by the customers. Shopping was sometimes a lengthy process, involving queueing up several times at different counters. 'Decimal day' was 15th February 1971.

Mike Hayes and Dave Owen wheel their transmitter through a Sutton park, in a pram, a few months after Radio Jackie was launched in 1969.

Transmitters made out of biscuit tins.

Radio Jackie – the pirate pop station

Radio Jackie first hit the airwaves during the early afternoon of 20th March 1969 at Mike Knight's home in Burleigh Road, off Stonecot Hill, Sutton. His mother, Mollie, ran the station and took telephone requests and after her son was arrested she used to go down to the police station and demand: "Release my boys. I'm not going until you've released them!"

The station, broadcast from crude equipment wheeled around fields in a pram, used to be part of the Helen broadcasting network which involved lots of little stations that went on air for just half an hour each, successfully avoiding detection by the Post Office.

Radio Jackie was broadcast from Burleigh Road for a few weeks before it went into the fields with the presenters using car batteries to power the equipment. The batteries and transmitter were wheeled across Surrey's wooded parks in an old perambulator.

Eventually, the station was on air all day on Sun-

days, being transmitted from secluded countryside at various locations including Jubilee Way, Tolworth; King George's Field, Tolworth; Berrylands sewage farm; Worcester Park, Epsom Downs and a field near Claygate Station. The lads, in their late teens, gave themselves the pseudonyms of Mike Knight, Dave Stevens and Dave Wright.

The enterprising young men used to play a real-life cat and mouse game with the PO radio investigators, 'Stan Smith' and Eric Gotts. On one occasion, Mike Knight was fined £15 and ordered to pay 10 guineas costs for illegal broadcasting. But the station survived and flourished until its last broadcast on 5th May 1985.

Meanwhile, another illegal station was providing a much-needed local service in Hook. Radio Telstar, was run by a skilful schoolboy from his home in Kelvin Grove, Hook. The Tiffin Boys' pupil used the Tornados' 1962 classic hit, Telstar, as the station's theme tune, before being raided by the Post Office inspectors and taken to court, where he was described as being of excellent character.

Operators in the new and modernised VIGilant exchange at Sutton. The picture was taken in May 1957 and is representative of the exchange in the early part of the 1960s. This new switchroom, which opened in April 1957, was blessed with auto-manual boards and replaced an earlier manual centre. In 1966, 'VIGilant' was replaced with 01-642 numbers. Fascinating glimpses of the early telephone system which has seen so many changes over the decades can be caught at the BT Museum next to Blackfriars Station in London. Admission is free.

Exchange names, not numbers

ELMbridge, LOWer Hook, VIGilant, CROydon

UP until March 1966, Surrey's suburban areas still used telephone numbers preceded by an exchange name.

Names like ELMbridge, UPLands, DERwent, KINgston, appeared on the top of stationery and shopfronts, indicating the three letters people had to dial before the standard four-figure telephone number. In March 1966, the names began to be phased out and replaced with 01 London numbers.

Most telephones in the '60s were made of black Bakelite and carried a plastic-covered paper disc in the centre which stated the number and also reminded users of the 999 number for police, fire or ambulance. The metallic dial with ten holes started with 1 and ended on 0. The initial hole only had 1 showing, and no letters. Hole 2 was also AB or C; hole 3, DEF and so on. The emergency numbers were printed in red ink. Sometimes a brown plaited cord would lead from the phone to the junction box, and more often than not, telephones were located in the coldest and most draughty parts of the home. It was unusual to find them next to the sofa or by the bedside.

The Old Exchange Names

Year introduced	Name	Area	01 (now 0181) number
1923	ADDiscombe	Addiscombe	01-654
1964	BLUebell	Addiscombe	01-656
1958	BYWood	Kenley-Purley	01-668
1965	COOmbe End	Malden	01-949
1884	CROydon	Croydon	01-688
1936	DERwent	Worcester Pk	01-337
1930	ELMbridge	Surbiton	01-399
1929	EMBerbrook	Dittons	01-398
1930	EWEll	Ewell	01-393
1937	FAIrlands	Sutton-Belmont	01-644
1960	FRAnklin	Wallington	01-669
1965	GALleon	Worcester Park	01-330
1965	IVYdale	Ewell	01-394
1893	KINgston	Kingston	01-546
1955	LOWer Hook	Hook-Chessington	01-397
1907	MALden	New Malden	01-942
1958	MELville	Sutton	01-643
1908	MITcham	Mitcham-Morden	01-648
1900	MOLesey	Molesey-Hampton	01-979
1958	MUNicipal	Croydon	01-686
1927	PROspect	Mortlake	01-876
1892 (pre)	RIChmond	Richmond	01-940
1931	SANderstead	Sanderstead-Selsdon	01-657
1923	THOrnton Heath	Thornton Heath	01-684
1935	UPLands	Purley	01-660
1937	VIGilant	Sutton-Belmont	01-642
1943	WALlington	Wallington-Carshalton	01-647

As from March 1966, all new and re-locating subscribers were given '01' numbers followed by the new three-figure exchange number and then the existing four-figure number. Some shopkeepers couldn't be bothered to pay out to change their shop front boards, and certainly Ace Autos in Ace Parade, Hook, was just one of the many commercial premises where the old exchange name LOWer Hook remained on show until the Eighties.

Elderly people also continued to answer the telephone, 'Elmbridge . . .' or similar, right into the next decade. Between January and September 1967, the remaining lines on the area's automatic exchanges were renumbered, and by the autumn of 1968, all of the old format numbers had disappeared from the telephone directories.

To make life simple, the Post Office allowed people to still use the lettered dialling, if they wished, for several years, and even in 1970, a quarter of calls were still being dialled with the old codes. Eventually, in 1972, it was no longer possible to dial any number by the old method.

The style of phone dial commonplace in the Sixties. It was usually displayed on black Bakelite telephones.

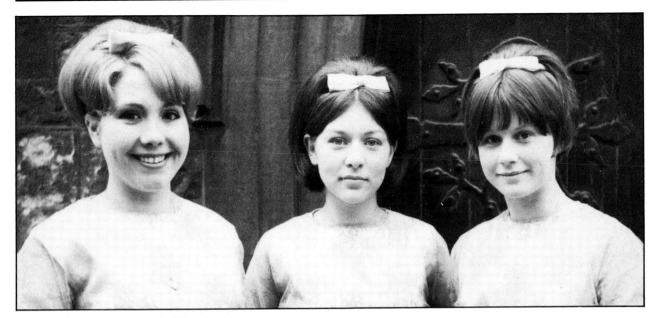

Bridesmaids at a wedding in March 1965.

Hairstyles of 1965

A heavy application of lacquer

THESE bridesmaids at a wedding near Croydon in 1965 show the hair fashions in vogue at the time. The wedding was on 6th March 1965, a cold day with snow showers. A few miles away in central London, Goldie, the escaped golden eagle swooped on a duck in Hyde Park.

The wedding was at St Mark's Church, South Norwood, where the vicar was Reverend Capper. A local band played 'I've Got My Love To Keep You Warm' in a bid to counteract the unseasonal chill in the air.

Bridesmaids Janet Anderson, Josephine Bush and Christine Bush, pictured left to right above, spent a long time on their hair to look good for the marriage of David Anderson to Anne Thomas of Cromer Road, Norwood.

Josephine recalled: "To get our hair looking like that we had to work from the back, forward, back-combing it all over, spraying it with heavy lacquer, waiting for it to dry, before smoothing the front bit over the back-comb and lacquering again."

At the time of the wedding, Josephine was 16 years old and was enjoying trips to Croydon's Fairfield Halls to see the Dave Clark Five and Herman's Hermits who had enjoyed a number one with I'm

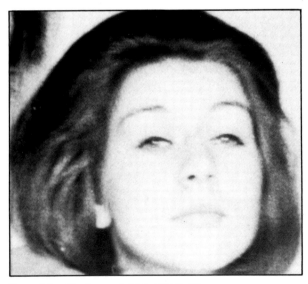

Josephine Bush aged 15 in 1963. She was forbidden from seeing the Rolling Stones in concert.

Into Something Good. The lively teenager, who was brought up by her grandmother in Cromer Road, was not into something good on one occasion when her guardian forbade her from seeing the Rolling Stones in concert.

Malden Road railway bridge, 1961, and an RF single decker bound for Sutton garage.

The view north up Malden Road, New Malden, 1961, with the RACS store and MacFisheries on the left.

Shop signs in the Apple Market, Kingston, circa 1961.

Beatnik Brigade giving teenagers a bad name

Kingston Upon Thames 1964

THE year 1964 began with the lure of Screaming Lord Sutch – 'the-almost-Member-of-Parliament' playing in The Cellar Club at 22a High Street, Kingston.

January 1964: Paper sacks replaced dustbins in the town area. They're more hygienic, Kingston Council believed. The scheme was to extend to the whole borough over the next seven years.

Big plans to expand Bentalls department store were announced.

Posters went up advertising a gig by Georgie Fame and the Blue Flames at the Kingston Baths, Coronation Hall, on 4th January. Tickets were 5s (25p) in advance. And Wayne Gibson was scheduled to perform at the Cellar Club on 24th January.

Eden Street Methodist Church was closed, but a new building was planned to replace it.

The Post Office said that the word Surrey should be kept in the postal address to avoid confusion when the town transferred to the Greater London boroughs in 1965.

Kingston College of Technology in 1967. Four years earlier, in March 1963, students from here began to form a small core of the Rolling Stones' first fans. They attended the Crawdaddy Club at the Station Hotel, Richmond, where dancing on table tops was encouraged by concert promoters.

Controversy raged over whether wrestling should be banned at Coronation Hall.

The *Surrey Comet's* fashion writer wrote that the Beatnik brigade "is probably to blame for teenagers generally getting a bad name over matters of dress and general appearance". Meanwhile, the snow and slush of early January had brought out a new trend in footwear . . . boots . . . "hundreds of them". The journalist observed: "Dozens of different styles appeared in the streets of Kingston, from neat fur-lined ankle-length foot warmers on the elderly and middle aged women to the oh-so-kinky creations in shiny leather favoured by the younger generation."

A 65 bus left the road outside the Fox and Goose public house in Petersham Road, Ham, and ploughed through five gardens. Fortunately no-one was injured.

In deck chairs, some housewives camped all night for bargains in the January sales at Wallis dress shop in Clarence Street. "I am the luckiest girl in Kingston," said one, after scooping a 23½gn coat for £5.

February 1964: The Rolling Stones and John Leyton gave two shows at The Granada, Kingston.

The Head of Hampton School of Commerce, Mr L. Jenkins, said: "The youth of today are not merely a crowd of beats and beatlemaniacs, but sensitive people who respond with true dedication and unselfish enthusiasm if offered better goods and higher ideals."

Major ring road plans for Kingston were unveiled in early February at the Guildhall. One hundred turned up including "a formidable display of objectors", said the *Comet*. The scheme included large scale development plans for Empire Engineering Works and a shopping precinct on a large area of land running north-south between the rear of both Clarence Street and Castle Street.

By 5th February all tickets for the Rolling Stones' concert at The Granada had sold out.

Kingston Tech students were among the Rolling Stones' first group of fans.

Children wave to the Queen as she leaves Kingston Grammmar School after her visit on 24th March 1961.

Twist, shake and rave at the Coronation Hall

Babies boom in Kingston

IN February 1964, the *Surrey Comet* reported that "for some unknown reason – maybe because it is becoming fashionable to have large families – twice the normal number of babies are expected to be born in the Kingston area during the next four months."

Home births were subsequently encouraged by medical officers who declared a state of emergency.

Meanwhile, on the exploding rock and pop scene, top Sixties' bands were taking Kingston by storm. The Yardbirds were booked to play at the Coronation Hall on 10th February and nine days later, "the country's foremost r and b group, The Animals were expecting crowds at The Cellar Club in the High Street.

Back at the Kingston Baths' Coronation Hall, posters tempted youngsters to 'Twist, Shake and Rave' to the Tornados on 15th February, while the Cellar Club proclaimed that The Nashville Teens, "one of the most exciting groups in the country today – and they are local – yes, it's the Nashville Teens", would be on stage on 23rd February.

March saw Joe Brown and Manfred Mann and Co booked for the Kingston Granada on the 4th, while The Zombies playing with The Cheynes at Kingston Baths proved an attraction on 29th February with seats costing 5s (25p).

The Kingston by pass at Hook in the early 1960s after the underpass opened by the Ace of Spades.

A modern flat at Hook for £4,550

Norbiton bus drivers threaten to strike

IN the early part of 1964, Norbiton bus garage crews at Kingston threatened to strike over the proposed re-routing of the green 418 bus between the Duke of Buckingham and Surbiton Station, saying that the 'green' drivers are being paid less than the 'red' drivers and that the greens would be invading red territory. But London Transport bosses argued that the 65 red bus 'well intruded' into green areas of Leatherhead. One hundred and forty people signed a petition in the Villiers Avenue area against the re-routing. In the event, the Norbiton strike did not materialise.

February 1964 also saw scores of char ladies treated to a special show at the Granada cinema in Kingston. They saw 'Ladies Who Do' featuring Harry H. Cor-

bett. Kingston's mayoress, Councillor W.J. Marshall "chatted to the many chars".

On 26th March 1964, Jerry Lee Lewis was scheduled to appear at the Cellar Club in Kingston High Street. The American star's early Sixties chart hits had included What I'd Say, which climbed to number 10 in May 1961; Good Golly Miss Molly and Sweet Little Sixteen.

If you were trying to buy property in the area, prices varied betweeen £4,550 for a modern, first-floor flat with pleasant open views of Hook, or £7,950 for a three-bedroomed choice detached house with Halycon space heating at Ditton Hill, Long Ditton. Renting at Surbiton cost around £6 a week for an unfurnished ground floor flat with two bedrooms.

Spring is in the air in 1964

A royal baby in Richmond Park

MARCH 1964 was a time to celebrate in Kingston when a Royal baby was born. Telegrams and gifts of flowers were sent to Thatched House Lodge in Richmond Park on the 1st, a few hours after it was announced that Princess Alexandra had given birth the previous day to a baby son. The baby was born just after midday on the last day of February and weighed 9lbs 6oz. The father, Mr Angus Ogilvy was present at the birth, setting a precedent for a Royal.

On Sunday, 1st March, he went to the morning service at Westminster Abbey, the Dean, Dr E.S. Abbott describing his attendance as a "natural and spontaneous act of thanksgiving". The Princess and Mr Ogilvy moved into Thatched House Lodge on returning from their honeymoon after their wedding at Westminster Abbey on 24th April 1963. Mr Ogilvy took a five year lease of the house from Clare, Duchess of Sutherland.

The County of Surrey Association of Flower Arranging Clubs sent blooms which were arranged by Mrs Morcombe White of Thames Ditton, a county judge.

Meanwhile, Kingston's swinging youngsters were looking forward to a show at The Granada, Kingston,

which featured some big names of the day: Dusty Springfield, Big Dee Irwin, and Bobby Vee. There were two shows in the same evening and tickets cost 5s (25p); 7s 6d (37p) and 10s 6d (52p).

A local beat group from the Kingston area called The Epics believed their big break was imminent after being invited to play in France. The band was led by a young man called Jeff Parker.

Weybridge area band The Nashville Teens were back in town on 8th March if anyone had any energy left after being lured to the town centre the previous evening to see The Pentagons who "rave, twist and certainly will excite you".

The Coronation Hall at Kingston Baths also enticed youth to see The Barron Knights with Duke d'Mond the same weekend. Four months later, the Barron Knights' first chart hit, Call Up The Groups, reached number 3 and was their biggest smash of the decade.

As if all this on top of the Searchers and Dusty wasn't enough to quell the district's musical appetite, Cliff Richard and the Shadows returned to the town after their successful show in 1963. They performed again at the ABC, Richmond Road for one night only on 2nd April 1964. The best tickets were 15s (75p).

Georgie Fame and the Blue Flames were to headline the new Kingston rhythm and blues club at Surbiton Assembly Rooms on 24th March. An added attraction of the venue was a licensed bar open from 8pm to 11pm and easy access by buses 65, 201, 281, 282, 283, 406 and 714. Although Georgie Fame had not yet had a hit record, by December 1964, he was to be at the top position in the hit parade with Yeh Yeh.

A three-year-old girl seen wandering along the Kingston by pass at night in her pyjamas was led to safety by Mr J. Furlonger and taken to Malden Police Station.

Shoppers in Kingston were surprised to see a hearse, complete with coffin and flowers in the Wood Street car park during the middle of a busy Friday in March 1964 while the driver stopped for lunch on his way from Bournemouth to London.

Also in the same month, six Middlesex girls, coming to Kingston for a cinema visit, went on a "wholesale shoplifting expedition" in which they stole a total of 90 articles from four stores.

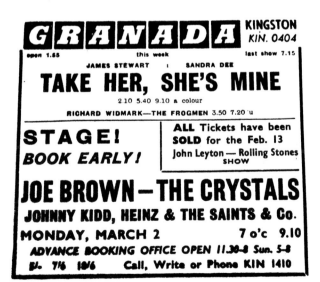

Da Doo Ron Ron and Then He Kissed Me had both been top ten hits for the Crystals in the year before their concert with Joe Brown at Kingston Granada on 2nd March 1964.

Hampton Court roundabout in April 1962. Trolleybus 667 starts back to Hammersmith 'Bdy' (Broadway). An Austin, Consul and Anglia also share the road.

A 602 destined for The Dittons, in Clarence Street, Kingston, about to enter Eden Street in April 1962. James Walker, the jeweller's is on the left.

A 605 trolleybus in Kingston Road, New Malden, in the summer of 1961.

Sad day in May 1962

End of an era for trolleybuses

THE early Sixties saw the end of an era for the trolleybus in Surrey.

Town centres at Kingston and Surbiton had their skylines woven with wires as the trolleybuses threaded their way through the streets, nourishing themselves on the overhead electricity supply. But these much-loved 'trackless' buses came to the end of their life in 1962.

When the wires were taken down, the operation was conducted at night to avoid inconvenience to people. After dark on 12th June 1962, an incident occurred in Eden Street, Kingston, when severed wires fell from their poles and whipped against plate glass windows at Kington's head post office, shattering the glass. And in London Road, falling wires damaged ten feet of neon light tubing and eight feet of lead roof on the canopy outside Messrs C & A Modes.

Former trolleybus driver Tom Norman of Long Ditton, later recalled several occasions when a trolleybus bound for the leafy terminus at The Dittons was driven in a boisterous manner through the Richmond Road-Clarence Street-Eden Street junction and the trolley booms bounced off the wires and smashed through the upper windows of the Wheelwrights public house. Apparently, this happened so often that bars had to be fitted to the windows.

Others remember a trolleybus catching fire as it hurtled along Ewell Road, Tolworth, with its roof ablaze as startled schoolboys fled to safety. One of those boys was Chris Leaney who remembered: "It was the most frightening moment of my life". Roof fires were not uncommon since there were irregular power surges, especially when the vehicles were overcharged in traffic jams and foggy conditions.

The last day of the trolleybuses in Kingston – 8th May 1962.

Introduced in 1931, the vehicles ferried millions of shoppers between Twickenham, Kingston, Surbiton, Tolworth and New Malden in the following three decades. But on 8th May 1962, the very last trolleybus ran in the district – and indeed, in London. A ceremonial journey was made by 'fans' on an original No 1 trolleybus brought out of a museum at Clapham for the occasion and put into use on a special run between Fulwell depot and Kingston. Hundreds of people gathered to watch the spectacle and the vehicle was bedecked with bunting for the event.

The very last trolleybus to run was No 1521, an L3 class trolleybus which ran from Wimbledon to Fulwell depot on route 604, on the night of 8th-9th May 1962. It was crowded with passengers and was followed by a procession of cars. "It was received by a cheerful, sentimental crowd at Fulwell," according to trolleybus expert Ken Blacker. Some of London's remaining 125 trolleybuses were sold to Spain and put into use for many years after.

Route numbers changed over the years, but in the last stages of the trolleybuses' life, Surrey communities in and around Kingston were served by the 601, 602, 603, 604 and 605.

The **601** ran from Twickenham to Tolworth. It started its journey behind the Tolworth Broadway, Ewell Road, terminating in the service road. It went along the Ewell Road to St Mark's Hill, down to Surbiton Station and along Claremont Road to Surbiton Crescent, Penrhyn Road, Kingston town centre, Kingston Bridge, Hampton Wick, Teddington and Twickenham.

The **602** started at the Dittons (Winter's Bridge), and went along Portsmouth Road to Brighton Road, Surbiton, then up Victoria Road to Surbiton Station, turning down Claremont Road and following the fixed wire route to Kingston before going along Eden Street, London Road, Park Road and Kings Road, looping back to Kingston via Richmond Road.

The **603** began at Tolworth (Red Lion) returning to Kingston and then along Richmond Road to Kings Road, Park Road, London Road and Eden Street before its return journey to Tolworth.

The **604** ran from Hampton Court to Wimbledon town hall via Norbiton, New Malden and Raynes Park.

Finally, the **605** ran from Teddington to Wimbledon, calling at bus stops in Hampton Wick, Clarence Street, Cambridge Road, Kingston Road, New Malden fountain, West Barnes Lane and Worple Road.

Sutton and West Croydon's trolleybuses were taken off the road around 1959.

The vehicles in Kingston were replaced by Routemaster buses such as those used on the 283 Kingston loop service.

Kingston in 1960 at the end of the trolleybus era. Note the two-way traffic in Clarence Street. Approaching is a 601 trolleybus destined for Tolworth. The "trackless trolleybus system" introduced in the early 1930s, came to the end of the line in Kingston in May 1962.

The 605 trolleybus to Malden and Wimbledon passes C&A in Kingston while a 604 to Hampton Court, advertising Chalet cheese, approaches on a sunny morning in 1960. Note the helmet-less scooter riders in the picture.

A 601 trolleybus to Tolworth, via Teddington and Kingston, sets off from Twickenham, in about 1960. Going the other way is a policeman on a motorcycle, wearing his regulation helmet.

A bamboo pole is raised outside Kingston Granada.

Carried under the chassis for emergencies

Bamboo poles were essential

A 601 Tolworth-bound trolleybus is being taken out of service in Clarence Street, outside The Granada Cinema in Kingston to allow other trolleybuses to pass. A bamboo pole is used by the conductor to move the trolley arms away from the wires.

A bamboo pole, measuring about 15 feet long, was always kept under the chassis of the trolleybus for use when the wires became detached or the vehicle needed to be taken out of service during mechanical breakdowns.

Shoppers recall with amusement stories of conductors fiddling around with the poles on busy days when trolleys became unhooked although this was not a frequent problem, trolleybus fans are quick to point out.

In the picture above, a 406a London Transport bus heads off to the country, passing C and A on the way, while a 265 from Chessington, Copt Gilders and Hook, draws nearer on its way to East Acton.

The Granada is showing A Pair of Briefs with an evening performance starting at 7pm. The date of this animated photograph is April 1962, when Wonderful Land by the Shadows was enjoying an eight-week spell at number one in the hit parade.

Although Kingston's trolleybuses were the last to run in London, they were also the first to be introduced in 1931. The reason they were still on the road so late as 1962 was that the original 'diddlers' had worn out by 1948 and were replaced by a new fleet which obviously had a further lifespan, outlasting others running in the capital.

Kingston on a Saturday in April 1962 – just weeks before the trolleybuses were removed from service. This was the Clarence Street junction with Eden Street.

A 601 trolleybus turns round the corner from Ewell Road, Surbiton into St Mark's Hill for the descent down to Surbiton Station in April 1962. It was destined for Twickenham.

The Rolling Stones in their early days. They played at Kingston, Sutton, Epsom, Guildford, Woking, and, of course, Richmond, during their arduous UK touring days of 1962-4.

An advert in the *Surrey Comet* announcing the Rolling Stones' appearance at Kingston Granada on 13th February 1964.

John Leyton, who shared a bill with the Stones when he came to Kingston Granada on 13th February 1964. In the summer of 1961 he enjoyed a number one hit with *Johnny Remember Me*.

Rolling Stones, Yardbirds, Animals, Joe Brown, Manfred Mann, Zombies, Dusty, Bobby Vee, Jerry Lee Lewis, Barron Knights, Searchers, Crystals and Cliff Richard — all in three months at Kingston.

Surrey mods on a scooter trip to the Isle of White. A teenaged cousin of Paul Garett is pictured with Parka-wearing fellow mod Jill Harvey. Paul, pictured right, later became a well known Surbiton hairdresser.

Scuffles outside a jazz club — but camaraderie best remembered

Molesey boys clash with Kingston mods

THE mod era was an exciting time for Surrey teenagers who had just bought their first scooter. Evenings would be filled with adventure and trips to the coast would be enjoyed at weekends when scores of riders would set off, helmetless, through the fresh air to meet like-minded boys and girls at seaside resorts such as Brighton and the Isle of Wight.

During the week, teams of mods would seek out the Surrey night spots and jazz clubs for entertainment. One of these was the Cellar Club in Kingston which first had its home in Ashdown Road, and then at 22a High Street. Groups of riders would also head off to places like the Wimbledon Palais to see bands like The Who.

When in Kingston High Street, the club was reached by way of steps up to a small ground level bar. Around 1964 local mods used to gather there to see bands like the Yardbirds, Animals, Nashville Teens and Checkmates.

One of those mods was Paul Garett, who later became a Surbiton hairdresser for more than 20 years in Victoria Road. He recalled: "Everyone got rid of their BSAs and bought a Lambretta. We used to go down to Kingston in our chrome-sided bikes and meet at the 'Jazz' Cellar. Everyone used to drink rum and blackcurrant; it was unbelievable. Although we were mods, two years earlier, we were rockers. I later had a lime green two-tone suit, which changed patterns in the different lights. You'd go to Burton's for your suit, but when it came to Parkas, you'd only buy ones which were ripped. We used to wear Hushpuppies when we were on our scooters. They were good times. I'd always make sure I had the best Lambretta scooter around.

Kingston mod Paul Garett who always boasted having the best scooter in town.

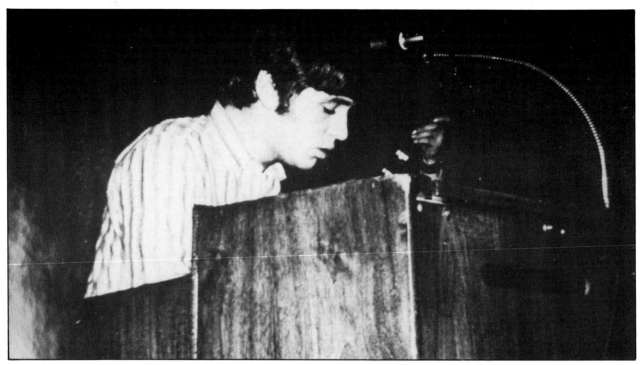

Georgie Fame playing at Kingston Polytechnic in early 1965 at one of the winter dances. He was at number one with Yeh Yeh at the time.

"There was a camaraderie you don't get today. There was no stabbing daggers in – even between the mods and rockers. Sometimes there was physical violence, though, and on one occasion, about 20 Molesey boys fought outside the Cellar Club near the Odeon with the Kingston boys but that was all. There were no dodgy dealings. The police station had not then been built in Kingston High Street and was still in London Road."

Mr Garett said his group of mods were led by 'The General', a man whose real name was Brian, because "he was the tallest and one of the toughest. If there was any trouble he was your man." The General was also described as a peacemaker who sorted out any disagreements.

The young folk also amassed at Kingston Baths where the best r and b bands of the time played, and the Toby Jug, where Mr Garett remembers the Drifters played in a small room. He said the girls would wear their hair like Sandie Shaw's. Another of the Cellar's attractions was Alan Price who had three top ten hits in the Sixties and other chart successes.

The mods frequently bought their machines from Chessington Scooters in Hook Road, Hook, near the Ace of Spades. This outlet was one of the main dealers of Lambretta and Vespa scooters in the area.

Peter Forsdick who worked at the shop for some 30 years after joining his family business in 1965 remembered the mods turning up in their droves on chrome-sided bikes bearing a variety of mirrors and lamps.

"We used to go to Brighton in groups of 20 or 25 in the days of mods and rockers and there used to be fights there," he said. "We'd go to various dances and the Orchid at Purley was a favourite. We also went to see The Who at Wimbledon Palais."

Nearer home, the friends would meet up in the Karenna Cafe in Hook Road and go into a back room that later formed part of the kitchen. Younger pals would meet at Surbiton Youth Club then in Langley Avenue where in later times the Police Federation headquarters moved to. Members recall news of the assassination of President John Kennedy breaking in November 1963 and being "stunned at the bus stop while waiting for a 65 back to Hook."

In 1971, Chessington Scooters was renamed Chessington Motorcycles and continued throughout the next quarter of a century to be one of the main dealers in the area.

Decades later, a 1950s Marconi wireless, still in working order, played music to customers and in a small measure, recalled fondly those vibrant times of Sixties youth.

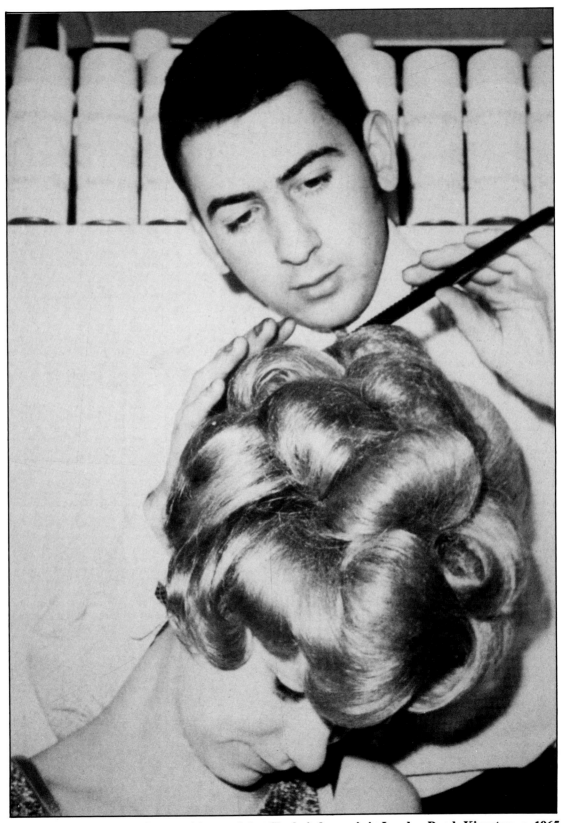

King of the mods – Paul Garett with a model at She hairdresser's in London Road, Kingston, c. 1965.

Fine Fare beneath Tolworth Tower, soon after its opening in 1964. It was proclaimed as being the biggest supermarket in Europe at the time. Posters in the window advertised PG Tips tea for 1/4½d (7p) a quarter.

BEFORE: Tolworth Odeon stood on the site of the tower. It shut in October 1959 and was demolished c.1960. The last film shown was I'm Alright Jack.

AFTER: Tolworth Tower was constructed in 1962-3 and for miles around became a visible landmark of Tolworth and a striking symbol of Sixties' skyscraper architecture with its 21 floors.

When Fine Fare opened in 1964, it lured staff away from other stores by offering 2s 6d (12½p) an hour. Doreen, above, was one of the first recruits.

Ruth Bardens was the sundae bar assistant at Fine Fare's huge new store beneath Tolworth Tower in 1964. She served many Rumbabas – doughnuts with a hole in the middle, soaked in a rum-like syrup with a blob of artificial ice cream.

Headlines from the *Surrey Comet* of 25th January 1964 following the Yardbirds' sensational appearance at the launch of the Surrey Rhythm and Blues Club at the Toby Jug, Tolworth.

300 mods, rockers and beats at launch

Rhythm and Blues Club, Toby Jug, Tolworth

ONE of Surrey's top music venues where young people could hear the best sounds of the Sixties was the Toby Jug at Tolworth.

In the vibrant function room, hundreds would gather to let their hair down to the best rhythm and blues music around.

The mood of those dizzy days at the pub, which stands next to a busy roundabout on the A3 beneath the Tolworth Tower skyscraper, is captured in an edition of the Surrey Comet dated 25th January 1964.

'Storming, shaking fans – 300 mods, rockers and beats who piled into the hall at the Toby Jug,

Tolworth, and 200 who did not get nearer than the door – assured instant success for Surrey's latest Rhythm and Blues Club and its young residents, The Yardbirds. The opening night on Monday was a sure-fire hit.

'If further proof were needed that rhythm and blues music has become the latest "with-it" rave, the hordes of youngsters who wiggled and shook, en-raptured, in the Toby Jug restaurant and ballroom certainly supplied it.

'The dark, vibrating "cavern" – impossible to recognise as a ballroom and restaurant – was, until recently, the home of a failing "trad" jazz club. Now,

A happening at the Toby Jug Blues

Jethro Tull playing at the Toby Jug, Tolworth, early in 1969, during the second rock and blues era in the pub's function room. Freelance photographer Graham Page took these photographs for the *Surrey Comet*, which reported: "Pop music clubs frequently suffer rowdyism, but the fans at the Toby Jug patronise it, it seems, solely for the pleasure that blues music gives them." The guitarist on the left is Jethro Tull's Glen Cornick who went on to form Bloodwyn Pig.

new life has been brought to it by the long-haired Yardbirds, who have an average age of under 20.

'Their music, belted out on hard-worked guitars, drums and mouth-organ – known to the initiated as a "harp" – is enhanced with the kind of rhythmic punch which is meted out by a provoked Sonny Liston.

'The group, professional performers for just six months, have worked in public and on records with the coloured American artist, Sonny Boy Williamson, at present touring Britain. The group's own first record will be released in Germany at the end of the month.

'Among the group's other qualifications are appearances at the Marquee Club, Oxford Street, and a performance on Wednesday at the Mecca of pop, the Cavern in Liverpool.

'Mr Len Fletcher, of Farnborough, Kent, who runs the club with a partner, was well satisfied with Monday's opening.

'Referring to his attempt to introduce "trad" to Tolworth at the end of last year, Mr Fletcher explained that "by the sixth week they were down to 60 people at the club".

'There seems little chance that this new venture will fail in the same way. In fact, the only disaster of the evening was a broken guitar string at the start of the finale number.

'"These things happen, even to the Beatles," announced Keith Relf, singer and "harp" player, and the group, one guitar short, romped through the finale, to the obvious and complete satisfaction of the clientèle.'

Looking down on the Toby Jug, right, and the construction work on the bowling alley in 1964. The picture was taken from the top of the newly-built Tolworth Tower skyscraper.

Led Zeppelin, Fleetwood Mac, Howlin' Wolf

Top bands at Tolworth, 1969

AT the time the Yardbirds played at the Toby Jug in 1964, the band's line-up was Eric Clapton (guitar), Keith Relf (vocals), Jim McCarty (drums), Chris Dreja (guitar) and Paul Samwell-Smith (guitar). Clapton, then aged 18, was born in Ripley, Relf, then 20, was born in Richmond and Dreja, then 17, in Surbiton. Clapton was in later times replaced by Jeff Beck and Samwell-Smith by Jimmy Page.

Page went on to form Led Zeppelin after the Yardbirds disbanded in 1968, and this hugely successful new band performed in its early days at the now famous Tolworth venue.

Acts of note to have played at the Toby Jug circa 1968-9 include: John Lee Hooker, Black Sabbath, King Crimson, Howlin' Wolf, Freddie King, Tim Rose, Peter Green's Fleetwood Mac, Bloodwyn Pig, The Keef Hartley Band, John Mayall's Bluesbreakers, Love Sculpture and Free.

Blues fan Stuart Andrews recalled: "You did not dress according to the temperature, you dressed to be a hit. At the very end of the Sixties, girls were wearing long velvet coats which almost touched the ground and boys would wear slim-fit shirts like a second skin." He added: "People seemed so emaciated and there were hardly any fat people."

He said the John Mayall act was memorable for band member Dick Heckstall-Smith playing two saxophones at once, each giving out a different tune. Also leaving a lasting impression was Mick Taylor's guitar-playing, which "was the most gripping you could ever hear. All the girls were potty about this baby-faced blond chap. The audience would stand there like druids, shaking and wobbling their heads to the lead guitar solos."

Promiscuous behaviour was common in the Sixties and some people recall an incident when a member of the audience vanished behind the heavy fire curtains during the performances to get to know a girlfriend better.

Pointer's still had a horse-drawn cart

Dual carriageway splits Hook

HOOK was split down the middle when a dual carriageway was built in 1962-3 and it lost much of its village-like flavour.

A large strip of gardens down the eastern side of the Hook Road were subject to compulsory purchase orders so the A243 could be widened between Ace Parade and Bridge Road. Land could not be used on the opposite side because of the cemetery in St Paul's Church, but trees and sunken, hedge-lined paths were lost near the recreation ground.

Hook's shops were small and friendly. Mrs Lineham, her white hair in a bun, sold toys and wool in Arcade Parade. The Maypole, on the other side, had square boxes with lids, some containing broken biscuits and the shop always had a strong smell of cheese. Shoppers had to read their lists out to the assistants or have the goods delivered by a grocery boy on a bicycle.

Bishops had a small pay-at-the-till store before its biggest branch was built on the site of the Homeware factory. Pointer's (later the Nat West Bank) was a grocer's and baker's and bread was delivered by horse-drawn transport as late as the Sixties. In the store, sugar was weighed and placed in blue bags, and a similar method was used for raisins, sultanas and dried fruit. The goods were weighed with brass scales and housewives were probably served by either a Mr Bill Bushell or a Mr Evans who lived in Somerset Avenue.

Bryant's was a 'sensible' clothes store stocking school uniforms for St Paul's, Lovelace, Tolworth Girls and others. Matthew's and J.S. Wood were the local butchers, and the two branches of A.C. Benn were the newsagents in the heart of Hook. One of Benn's kind hearted lady assistants used to feel sorry for some schoolboys and handed them a 6d Cadbury's bar which she would pay for out of her own money.

Sainsbury's at the Ace had long counters either side with a tiled floor and walls. Shoppers paid over the counter and items were individually wrapped. The eggs were in a basket on the counter. Bacon was sliced to order.

The Ace also had a small coffee shop, The Ace teashop with little wooden tables. The cafe was nicely kitted out with oak furniture. Ladies looking for classy day and evening wear may have visited Lanselle's, and had their hair 'done' at Vogue's in Arcade

a lædybird lernin tw reed bok
helpin at hœm
bie M. E. GAGG, N.F.U.

St Paul's School, Hook, was just one to try out a new teaching system designed to help infants learn 'tw reed' more easily in the late 60s. The scheme was later abandoned owing to confusion.

Parade. The RACS supermarket in the same parade had thick, blue plastic shopping baskets and had several departments housed in smaller units.

In the early days of the 1960s, the 265 bus ran to Copt Gilders, later to be replaced by the 65A. If you had a cycle you would probably go to Sidney Grove's at Ace Parade for repairs.

With little traffic on the roads, the sound of Chessington Zoo's lions roaring at night could be heard from as far away as Bramham Gardens – at least a mile away.

St Paul's School, like many others in the region, still handed out corporal punishment in the first part of the decade, and occasionally as late as 1969. Two nine year old boys received a stroke on the hand in October 1961 for taking and defacing a hymn book. And four boys were rewarded with three strokes on the seat a month later by the school headmaster for 'running around the cloak room after being warned'. The last recorded punishment was a stroke on the hand for two boys accused of misbehaviour in the dining hall and insolence in October 1969.

Cliff Richard meets fans and cinema staff at his concert in Kingston's ABC on 7th March 1962.

Cliff Richard and Shadows storm Kingston ABC

CHANTING queues, souvenir touts and traffic jams greeted the arrival in Kingston on Wednesday 7th March 1962 of 'Britain's leading pop singer', Cliff Richard who made two personal appearances in shows at the ABC Cinema.

The *Surrey Comet* said: 'Needless to say, there were no seats at either show though there were a surprisingly large number filled by mums and dads. Whether they went of their own free will or merely to ensure that their offspring did not get trampled in the rush is not certain.'

Obviously somewhat overwhelmed by the concert, the newspaper's critic wrote: 'Compère Tony Marsh, obviously an old hand at dealing with predominately teenaged audiences, provided an amusing line in smooth patter between the acts.

'Sustained, ear-piercing shrieks greeted the appearance of the Shadows, reproduced every time any of their three guitarists lifted their feet, bent their knees or swayed their hips. Their rendering of FBI

nearly brought the house down.

'The ovation given to Cliff Richard was in fact so tumultuous that it was impossible to hear a single word of his first song.

'Undoubtedly, this 21-year-old singer has looks, charm, a melodious voice and a bundle of talent. He seems incredibly unassuming and yet more professional with each public appearance.

'It's a pity that his more gentle love songs were ruined by members of the 'see who can scream in the quietest part' clan. He is bouncing with rhythm every minute he is on stage; a dynamic personality. But oh, those screams.

'Cinema staff were on hand to ensure that no-one got over enthusiastic and tried to clamber on to the stage.

'Final impressions were of moon-struck girls in the front rows frantically throwing embroidered hearts on to the stage before the curtain came down.'

Chessington mods Barry Simner and Sandra Hendricksen on an outing to Winey Hill, Chessington, c.1965.

In **January 1964**, plans were unveiled for an American-style drive-in cinema with room for 700 cars at Chessington Zoo. The scheme, which would have been the first of its kind in Britain, was proposed by the zoo in conjunction with ABC Cinemas. It did not go-ahead. Surbiton Council turned down the application in March 1964.

Meanwhile, the same year, other things were on people's minds. Chessington County Girls School announced it was to close with the girls being moved to Fleetwood School in Chessington. Later that month, 40 staff at the Siebe Gorman factory in Davis Road, Chessington, staged a sit-down strike in protest at plans to shed more than a third of the workforce.

In **March 1964**, it was announced that Chessington Zoo's new keeper was Edward Orbell of West Road, Malden Rushett, who succeeded Jack Young who had emigrated to Australia earlier in the year.

Teenaged girls used to flock to Chessington Youth Club on Thursday night and perform slow aerobics to the accompaniment of a 'wonderful' pianist called Beryl. The club, run by the League of Health and Beauty, had the youngest membership in the country. It was a real social occasion for Chessington's young ladies.

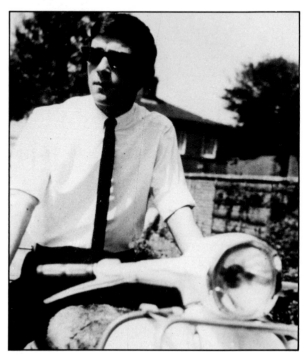

Mod Chris Isley, pictured near Southborough Boys School, Hook, where pupils in their last year were permitted by headmaster Mr J. Giddey to bring in their scooters. Chris's was a G.T. model.

Carefree days at Chessington Youth Club c. 1965.

A swarm of Lambretta scooters 'bristling with chrome'

Jiving at Chessington Youth Club

CHESSINGTON had a thriving youth club in the Sixties with a large contingent of mods as its members. Teenaged boys and girls nearly always arrived at the R.B. Loveless Hall in Church Lane on their prized Lambrettas, wearing parkas, some with fox tails attached to their hoods and coiled aerials wavering on the back of their bikes.

On Friday nights, dances would be held with local groups playing live music and the road outside would be full of chrome scooters.

Former youth club member Graham Page reminisced years later: "When the dance was over, the whole of Church Lane was full of scooters all the way to Bridge Road. Everyone would get half a pint at the

Blackamoor's because they were not too strict in there. Sometimes, as many as 50 scooters would go down Church Lane like a swarm of bees. The old people opposite the club would go crazy. They were wonderful days. They'll never be recreated. The car park was bristling with chrome."

He recalled buying a fire-damaged Lambretta in a panel-beater's yard near Southborough School, Hook, for just £3, doing it up, and riding it up and down the back alleys of Moor Lane.

The club was run for many years by George Nightingale and his much-praised helpers, Avice Land and Carol – who became Mrs Carol Barella of Raeburn Avenue, Berrylands. She was just 20 in 1965 when

Chessington Youth Club members Barry Simner and Sandra Henricksen in late 1966.

she became the club's voluntary leader and remained with the club until 1994. She said: "We were a lot more innocent in the Sixties than now and never thought about the dangers when going out."

She remembered that when the youth club was built, the floor was made of wooden blocks and dancing was prohibited because of the potential damage from stiletto heels. Instead, youths were allowed to dance on the stage. She said that coffee, tea and milk shakes were served in the club's Jack's coffee bar and as many as 200 would turn up for the Friday and Saturday dances to jive and rock'n'roll.

Before they hit the big time, the Dave Clark Five and Georgie Fame played at the club and a visit was made on one occasion by David Essex on a motorbike. His aunt apparently lived at Tolworth. The mods were filmed at one stage by a producer from Chessington.

On another occasion there was an incident near the Blackamoor's and several club members were

arrested and appeared in court but their leader made sure they were proved innocent.

Ex-members of the club remember with fondness coach trips to Brighton, a two-week holiday to Switzerland for £33, club football matches on Churchfields recreation ground, soccer excursions to Belgium, with girls invited; plus an aerobics class run by the League of Health and Beauty, which attracted girls as young as 14.

Occasionally, visiting mods or rockers would turn up from places like Redhill and trouble broke out, but it was not frequent. Rivalry between neighbouring towns in the 60s was put down to the fact that limited transport meant 'bus loads' of youths arriving en-masse and making locals feel somewhat intimidated. This sort of pattern does not happen today, Mrs Barella felt.

The club was named after R.B. Loveless, a former headmaster of Fleetwood School, Garrison Lane, which later became Chessington Community College in the 1980s.

Chessington mod, Steve Andrews, pictured next to Brighton Pier in 1965. His home was in Church Lane, where the buzz of dozens of scooters could be heard on Friday and Saturday nights.

A busy market day afternoon in Epsom, under the clock tower.

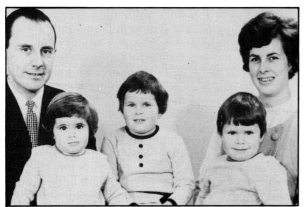

Residents Association in power

Mr Michael Arthur, aged 30, won the Ewell by-election in November 1966, representing the Residents Association. The voting was 695 (RA) and 256 for the Liberal candidate, Mr T.S. Grant. As a consequence, Epsom and Ewell Council's political balance remained unchanged with 36 RA members and four Labour. The winner, Mr Arthur was a key figure in Ewell, being a scout and Rover Scout and also chairman of the Ewell RA. He lived at Langton Avenue, Ewell, and was the father of three girls and a baby son. He was a director of the building firm, Bradley and Arthur.

Epsom's Derby race winners

Year		Horse
1960	—	St Paddy
1961	—	Psidium
1962	—	Larkspur
1963	—	Relko
1964	—	Santa Claus
1965	—	Sea Bird II
1966	—	Charlottown
1967	—	Royal Palace
1968	—	Sir Ivor
1969	—	Blakeney

IN the 1960s, the Epsom Derby was a big day out for the whole country. Around half a million people used to flock to Epsom Downs for the races and the fair with its assortment of 'real' gipsies offering fortune telling and other services. Even the schools had a day off. In 1962, all the favourites fell over at the Tattenham Corner bend. In 1964, Santa Claus won by about 11 lengths. St Paddy in 1960 was ridden by Piggott.

Epsom jockey Duncan Keith with his wife and children at their Banstead home in April 1965, after he had won the 2,000 Guineas race.

Runaway colt jumped over car

Epsom Derby 1965

ALTHOUGH favourite Sea Bird II (7-4) romped home in the sunshine Derby in June 1965, two Epsom horses were tipped locally to be the first past the post.

One of them, Niksar, was ridden by jockey Duncan Keith, aged 27, of Banstead who had won the 2,000 Guineas race in April that year. The other was I Say (28-1) who came third. Both Niksar and I Say were from the same Epsom stables.

Bad weather had plagued the Derby festivities in the run up to the big day and the previous Sunday had seen the lowest crowd for 20 years according to London Transport chiefs who had laid on extra buses up from the town. And on the same day, a fire had broken out in the enclosure of the Brigade of Guards, damaging 120 square feet of canvas.

Tumidora, a three-year-old colt in the last race at Epsom on Tuesday, 1st June, dashed down Chalk Lane, along South Street and ended up in the forecourt of the Marquis of Granby public house.

Before being held by Mr Arthur Surridge, a 57-year-old ex jockey who was passing by, the colt jumped over a car and gave the owner, Mr Robert Gamble, 23, of Kendor Avenue, Epsom, a fright. Mr Surridge, of West Hill, Epsom, told the *Epsom Herald*: "I slipped off the belt of my raincoat and with some tea cloths I got from a butcher's shop next door, made a sort of halter." The colt suffered a bruised shoulder and when rescued by mounted police, was led back to the stables.

Epsom's Mrs Smith, a Romany who foretold of King Edward VIII's abdication, had earlier said she could see the French horse Sea Bird with its nose first past the winning post.

Gary McGrath, a 13-year-old Epsom schoolboy from Longmead County Secondary, became a bit of a showbiz star in 1965.

In 1964, he played in the West End musical, Oliver, for nine months and then became much in demand. In July, 1965, Independent Television announced that viewers had selected him as the winner of his heat in the Silver Star contest in the children's programme show. He won the affection of the home audiences for his Cockney impressions in the Flash Bang Wallop song.

Gary attended a stage school at Ewell in rare moments of spare time brought about by being in constant demand to appear at various functions. The telephone was constantly ringing in his East Street home, Epsom.

A Ford Consul negotiates the roundabout at the top of the High Street, Epsom, circa 1964. In the background, leading up to South Street, are a parade of shops which include Mortimer's, the chemists; Derek Boyt the butcher; King and Rose (Reigate) Ltd.; Elspeth; Stebbing's the tobacconists; the Epsom Paint Stores and Richard Dearing, estate agents. The advertisement states: Beanz Meanz Heinz.

Traffic in Epsom queues up at the lights near the Spread Eagle Pub c.1964. The pub became offices in the 1980s. Reid's department store had several floors which shoppers could browse around – reached by way of a lift.

Numbers 94-96 High Street, Epsom, c.1964, which then housed Wright's café-restaurant-coffee lounge; a small furniture store; John Cornell hair fashions (open until 8pm, Thursdays and Fridays), and Barbara's the florists. The buildings survived the bulldozer over the next few decades.

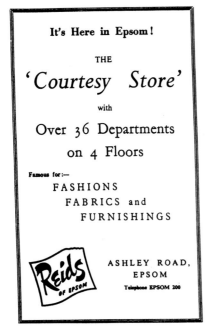

An advert for Reid's, where Epsom's shoppers enjoyed browsing.

An advertisement in February 1963 for Farm Garage, Church Street, Epsom, where the Zephyr was in vogue.

Sutton High Street, looking north from the Cock crossroads in 1962.

Concrete buries the past; farewell to the quaint tearooms

Old Sutton is bulldozed

Perched on the northern edge of Surrey, where the county's chalk downlands dwindle into the spacious gardens of suburbia, Sutton faced a dramatic change in the Sixties like every outer London borough.

It adopted a new, more imposing identity. As one of the new 32 Greater London boroughs born out of the 1965 boundary reorganisation, this leafy backwater which inspired the 1940s' radio serial, Mrs Dale's Diary – the daily account of a doctor's wife and her family – was about to challenge neighbouring Croydon as a commercial and shopping centre.

But sadly, those who recognised its attractive potential, closeness to the A217, London and two airports, imposed wholesale destruction of its quaint character.

Bulldozers savaged scores of mellowed red-brick old Victorian, Edwardian and 1920s buildings. For the developers had moved into Sutton to cash in on the building boom.

The commercial carnage changed the face of central Sutton as it did also in similar 'dreaming suburbs'.

Local landmarks like the Cock Tavern, an old coaching inn which stood at the town's main crossroads, suddenly disappeared to be replaced by a monolithic office block. Other rows of old shops, once the home of family businesses, butchers, haberdashers and similar, went with it.

The residential areas which suffered the most were those close to the shopping centre. South Sutton, where once the town's businessmen had their homes complete with maids and coachmen, was transformed for the worse.

Large old villas covered with creeper and ivy were bulldozed indiscriminately. Their original family occupants long gone, sold by their successors into the hands of property landlords, they had fallen into multi-occupation and disrepair. Families who remained were offered sums so attractive they couldn't refuse.

None of the buildings had any historic claim to conservation protection and there was no-one to preserve them. In later decades, the conservation movement

The site of The Cock pub in Sutton after demolition and clearance in April 1961.

which ironically grew out of the caring public's disgust with the architectural and development savagery of the Sixties, would have fought to save them. But these people had not yet formed ranks. The properties themselves were often so badly afflicted by neglect, the town hall planners nodded instant permission to their executioners.

Planning laws, now environmentally sympathetic, seemed unconcerned about the effect slabbed concrete replacements would have on environments. So, with swift sweeps of bulldozers and JCBs, the old houses of Mulgrave, Cavendish, Grange and Worcester Roads, together with those of Brighton Road and Woodcote Road, Wallington, were gone for good.

Years later, the officers running what was then a Tory controlled council, discovered how foolish their destruction had been, not in sentimental but practical terms. For, on the site of where once stood one home with one or two lavatories were blocks of a dozen or more homes each with a loo. And Victorian sewers supporting the borough's effluent couldn't stand the strain on the drains. The seriousness of the error was not fully evaluated until the next decade. Then, an emergency moratorium, a ban on any more mass home-building was imposed until several sewers could be reinforced.

Meanwhile, bastions of shopping centres which so far survived, continued to serve a social pattern of people, ranging from elderly gentlefolk, many of them retired from the colonies, to prosperous working class families.

The days of many of these shops were numbered either by development, the recession of the Seventies, or, as in the case of Shinners, the town's department store, by being swallowed up by a larger company.

Shinners, where once the minor aristocrats of Surrey, and the wives of rich traders, were ferried in by chauffeurs to buy bombazine fabric for their dresses, was renowned more for quality than style.

A family firm, Shinners changed little in the Sixties – the departments a muddle on three floors, the ground a series of 'steps' because of the steep gradient of the High Street where it stood.

A visit to the store was invariably followed by lunch or tea in the top floor restaurant. No trendy title or popular music – just a large room full of tables with spotless white tableclothes where meals were served by waitresses accompanied by a tinkling piano.

The 'swinging Sixties' failed to impress the range of Shinners' stock or its surroundings. The outrageous

New Hillman Imp at Sutton

The Phoenix Garage at Vale Road, Sutton, advertising the new Hillman Imp in 1963. The Tudor Cafe is across the road next to which is an advertisement for the Granada Cinema in the town.

The Cock in April 1960 soon to be demolished and William Pile, bookseller and stationer, on the corner of Carshalton Road and the High Street, Sutton.

fashions or loud music were not making much of an impression on the rest of the suburb so far, either.

If you didn't finish your shopping trip at Shinners you went to Fullers. One of the branches of this now-defunct chain of tea shops renowned for its walnut cake stood next to Irene Shaw's boutique at the Cock crossroads, where the old sign from the demolished pub is the only reminder of its existence.

Rene Shaw's was a renegade in a High Street stodgy with outfitters and ladies' wear retailers. It was a microcosm of what was going on in the King's Road complete with music, eye-catching windows and assistants wearing what horrified elderly ladies looking in the door described as "pelmets round their bottoms". These teenage girls tried the thigh-high skirts, cutaway dresses, mods and rockers' styles, and jewellery. They would be togging themselves out for a night out. This would invariably be in neighbouring Croydon, 'up West' or Streatham.

Many youngsters from roads in the stockbroker belt of Cheam and Wallington looked to friends from similar backgrounds – tennis clubs, the Young Conservatives and churches – for their compact social life.

The phrase 'who's for tennis' could have been coined in Sutton. Although the standard of play wasn't Wimbledon, the partying was enthusiastic.

Many churches had an active social life. The Young Conservatives reigned supreme in the Sixties as *the* social arena in which young people met partners who, with them, would perpetuate the lifestyle pattern set by parents. This provided comfort, large houses, private schools and security. These youngsters therefore, mixed little with those from the St Helier estate, the sprawling council development between Sutton and Morden.

The estate's small homes, identical to those in Welwyn Garden City, were a suitable class complement to the owner-occupier houses in the rest of the borough. Children and their occupants, many of them descendants of families who moved out of inner London when the estate was completed in 1937, were exploring the attractions of swinging London, going up to town on the nearby Northern line at Morden.

For older pupils, the area's amateur dramatic and operatic societies provided a social life. Productions of shows like The Boy Friend, Salad Days and Oklahoma were regularly staged.

The venues included Sutton Public Hall, where Noel Coward was said to have first performed as a

The Granada Cinema, Sutton, advertising the Countess From Hong Kong as a forthcoming title. It closed on 20th September 1975. Built in 1934 it had seating for 2,200.

My girdle's killing me . . . but the new Playtex golden girdles guaranteed a 'new, slimmer, smoother line' and were available at 84/- (£4.20) in 1963 from Shinners Ltd, Sutton High Street (Telephone VIG 6000).

A 1961 picture of Sutton Central Library at Manor Park House. It was demolished fifteen years later.

The entrance passage to Cheam junior Library, Park Lane, pictured in April 1961. On the left is a tea and coffee house and on the right C.E. Rowe's newsagent's. Outside, the Evening News billboard is luring prospective purchasers with its coverage of premium bond winning numbers. The Sutton and Cheam Herald, with a gothic-style type for its title, is displayed in the newspaper rack outside, next to the Lyons Maid ice cream board.

Comedian Jimmy Tarbuck makes a special appearance at Sutton's Granada Cinema c.1963. The streets were lined with hundreds of his fans.

child, and Carshalton and Wallington public halls. To watch professionals, the public went to the Granada Cinema which stood opposite the Police Station in Carshalton Road. This survived until the Seventies, but in the Sixties was the scene of packed houses for touring productions of major musicals, ballet, pop music, and big band concerts. An office block housing Securicor later stood on the spot which once echoed to the screams of girls swooning at Sixties' pop idols.

Up the road, the Top Rank Cinema building at Rosehill, survived the 60s' bulldozers, but changed later to a bingo hall. A memento of its days as a cinema remains with ghostly music from the long-since removed organ eerily being reported at times from residents in a nearby block of flats.

Buildings like the Public Hall and Shinners were swallowed up by the huge Allders store group who re-named the shop; building a huge store in the years to follow at the St Nicholas shopping complex.

Scores of elderly ladies with fur coats, blue rinses and leather handbags would lunch in the sprinkling of small restaurants where dishes like liver and bacon or shepherd's pie were always on the menu. Their favourite was a tea room where Sutton Post Office later stood in Grove Road. They would gossip and then go back to home in one of the many mansion

blocks of flats near to the station, or a large house where many lived on their own.

The new Sutton Council was establishing itself. With a Tory MP – the late Sir Richard Sharples – the area seemed destined to remain Tory forever. Little did anyone guess then that the breed of young 'meritocrats' growing amongst the ranks of some middle class children would eventually produce a Liberal MP, local boy Graham Tope who took the seat briefly in the Seventies before losing it to Tory Neil, later Sir Neil, Macfarlane who retired in the early 1990s. The council's buildings were then a smat-tering of premises around the area with its 'town hall' – a picturesque but inadequate red brick building in the High Street. This, too, was demolished in the Sixties.

Sutton's schools were a representative of its social mix – four grammar schools for high-flyers, and a number of small, ill-equipped and badly housed build-ings for the rest. It was many years before the latter were improved.

In the Sixties, Sutton was just coming out of its 'dreaming suburb' slumber. Although what it woke up to was advancement but at the cost of losing much of its heritage.

ODEON   GUILDFORD

Gen. Manager: E. J. Rowlings

FRIDAY, 21st JUNE, 1963

6.15 p.m.   TWO PERFORMANCES   8.30 p.m.

John Smith presents

THE BEATLES

"Please, Please Me"   "From Me To You"

plus THE JIMMY CRAWFORD PACKAGE SHOW

Lance Fortune - Jimmy Crawford - The Messengers
The Vampires - Rocking Henri - The Hayseeds
The Vikings with Michael London
VIC SUTCLIFFE compere

Seats: 10/- 7/6 6/6. Bookable in advance from Box Office, Odeon, Guildford. Tel. No. 4990. Orders by Post, please send remittance and s.a.e. State first or second performance, as required.

An advertisement which appeared in the *Leatherhead Advertiser* in 1963.

Tickets ranged from 6/6 to 10 shillings

Beatles at Guildford Odeon

THE Beatles played in the present day Surrey county only once – at Guildford Odeon on 21st June 1963, in the week their second hit single, From Me To You, had just slipped off the top of the hit parade after seven weeks in the number one position.

Tickets for the Friday night's two performances sat 6.15pm and 8.30pm cost 6s 6d (32½p) for the cheapest seats and 10s (50p) for the best seats.

Also on the bill were Lance Fortune, Jimmy Crawford, The Messengers, The Vampires, Rocking Henri, The Hayseeds, The Vikings and Michael London. The show was compared by Vic Sutcliffe.

Earlier, on 21st March 1963, the Beatles played at West Croydon's ABC cinema, where they supported Chris Montez. At the time, they had only had one major hit, Please Please Me, which had reached number 2 the previous week. Montez had a huge hit the previous autumn with Let's Dance.,

The only other hit was Love Me Do which had climbed to number 17 at its highest the previous October. So it was little wonder that the girls outside the cinema were not yet screaming for the Beatles, but for Chris Montez. Rumour has it that the Beatles heard the din and looked through the window, believing all the fuss was over themselves, and were disappointed to find it was for Montez instead.

Nevertheless, things had improved considerably since their show in Aldershot a few months earlier when only 18 paying guests turned up.

Beatles were the support act

The Beatles were billed as a support act to Chris Montez at the ABC Croydon on Thursday 21st March 1963. It is rumoured the Beatles were disappointed when they heard girls screaming outside and discovered the fuss was not over them but Chris Montez whose hits, Let's Dance and Some Kinda Fun had been top ten smashes just months earlier. This seems an unlikely tale according to a member of the audience at that show. Dave Lashmar who, when older, ran Beanos record collectors shop in Surrey Street, Croydon said: "I remember an awful lot of screaming, I can't recall any girl screaming for Chris Montez." He also recalled: "I didn't think that much of the Beatles. I had one of their albums which was more rock and roll, but when they were on, they performed their own songs and I didn't like them as much as the rock and roll."

Mansion of 27 rooms and psychedelic caravan outside

John Lennon moves into Weybridge

Kenwood at Weybridge where John Lennon lived.

DURING the Beatles' heyday, 23-year-old John Lennon moved to a very large house at Weybridge.

Kenwood was a 27-roomed mock-Tudor 'Hansel and Gretel' type mansion on top of salubrious St George's Hill. He bought it for £20,000 and spent twice this sum doing up the property and installing a heated swimming pool.

The book, The Lives of John Lennon, by Albert Goldman, paints an interesting image of his recluse-like life at Kenwood, when he was not touring.

He had been recommended by financial advisers that it would be beneficial to own such a property for tax reasons, but two years later he said he didn't feel at home in Weybridge and he wouldn't be stopping there for long.

At a party to celebrate the Beatles' forthcoming tour of America in 1964, Cynthia Lennon mentioned mistakenly to a friend that the house they were moving to was 'in Sunbury'.

One of the ornaments in the house was a suit of armour with a gorilla's head on top. This came from a gorilla suit he sometimes wore to keep warm! The Lennons had one of the first colour televisions on the market and this was placed in the grate of the fireplace where John would stare at the tube late at night, as if it was a real fire with pictures in the flames.

John hated the dining room which had been prepared with mauve felt over which hung paintings of vegetables which he gladly offered to a visitor who curiously admired them.

When they moved in, Cynthia couldn't get the modern-style cooker to work and a man had to be brought in from London to show her which switches to turn. The couple lived for nine months in an attic room while the huge restoration programme was embarked upon. In fact, even after this re-fit, they only lived in a small part of the house; John spending much time in a glassed-in extension overlooking a sloping terraced garden. The extension was decorated with Beatle awards and memorabilia. He spent long hours flaked out on a Queen Anne sofa, with his head on pillows, gazing at the TV with the sound turned off.

Also sharing the house was the Lennon couple's young son, Julian, who attended Heath House Infants' School and grew up to be a noted musician. Cynthia's mother, Lil Powell, also stayed for prolonged periods.

In the book, The Beatles, the authorised biography by Hunter Davies (1968), the author states that John also kept a psychedelically painted caravan in the grounds, which was colour co-ordinated to match the patterns on his painted Rolls Royce.

"He has a full-time gardener, a housekeeper called Dot and a chauffeur called Anthony. None of them lives in. 'Ant' or Dot usually answer the front door although sometimes John does, but he rarely answers the telephone.

"It is almost impossible to get him on the phone because he has an answer-phone system which takes messages. This in itself puts off most people trying to get through to him. There's a recorded voice which says "This is Weybridge 4,5 Wubblewoo, dubblewoo, please leave your message now. His ex-directory number is always being changed."

George, meanwhile, resided in nearby Esher, with his girlfriend, Patti Boyd, a young model, in a white bungalow 'furnished in the clean, modern style of Habitat', according to Albert Goldman's book.

After John had set up home in Weybridge, Ringo Starr followed suit, and lived with his hairdresser wife, Maureen, and young son Zak, in a large house at the foot of the hill on which Kenwood stood. He had a sunken garden built and also a cosy little pub constructed, called the Flying Cow, in which he spent quite a bit of time.

Paul McCartney was the only Beatle who did not set up home in Surrey.

At the time, Ringo lived at Sunny Heights, a mock-Tudor 1920s house at St George's Hill, Weybridge. He paid £37,000 for it but spent £40,000 doing it up. The huge wooded gardens sloped down to an ampitheatre dug out of the ground, but there was no swimming pool. There was, however, a playhouse in one of the large trees.

Harrison's Esher home

After moving to Surrey in the mid Sixties, when fame brought them fortunes, Harrison, Starr and Lennon lived in luxury. George had a single-storey bungalow in a very secluded and wooded estate owned by the National Trust at Esher. His bungalow had two wings which enclosed a courtyard and swimming pool.

Hunter Davies' 1968 book, The Beatles, says: "All the outside walls of the house have been painted by George, or at least sprayed in bright luminous-looking colours and from his gardens, the house looks like a psychedelic mirage."

Another anecdote Davies told was that when Harrison answered the phone he was heard to say gruffly: "Esher Wine Store? Sorry, No Sorry", before hanging up impatiently.

Beatles' Surrey performances

21st March 1963	West Croydon ABC
25th April 1963	Croydon Fairfield Hall
21st June 1963	Guildford Odeon
7th September 1963	Croydon Fairfield Hall

Other dates:

14th April 1963	Watched Stones play at Station Hotel, Richmond.
22nd February 1964	Beatles return to UK from States. Hysteria at London Airport.
23rd February 1964	Screaming fans' hysteria at Teddington Studios.

Beatlemania at Teddington — braving a trip to Esher Embassy

Hysteria over 'Fab Four'

A crowd of excited teenagers – more than 500 – besieged the ABC TV studios in Teddington, all day on Sunday 23rd February 1964 when The Beatles went there to record a show to be screened the following week.

Three girls were injured and had to be treated by three of the 30 policemen on duty at the studios on the banks of the Thames opposite Kingston. One police constable sustained injuries to his hands when he was crushed by the pressing crowds into a barrier gate.

The Beatles arrived at the studios in a launch. The *Surrey Comet* took up the rest of the story in an out-of-breath report: "At one stage, the locked gates were in danger of being broken down and had to be reinforced with wooden props.

"At one time, 50 Beatles fans were inside the compound undeterred by high security fences. They'd either climbed the fence or hoisted themselves from boats moored in 15 feet of water which they clung to while clambering to a river-facing wall.

"One girl fainted in the crowd. Then, a girl aged 16 – Sandra Simms – who works at the LCC children's home at Miles Lane, Cobham, made a swallow dive into the open vintage Rolls Royce in which the Beatles were being driven around the studio compound. Wearing placards reading 'George I love you' and 'Our Beatles are home, yeahh yeah yeah', she landed on the lap of her idol George Harrison. She was removed, her high red boots flailing, by security men and a policewoman, who took her to Teddington police station to calm down.

"In the afternoon, she was back, but fell from a fence and grazed her knee. She was taken to the studio first aid post for treatment and while there, her hand went through a window. She then had to be taken to West Middlesex Hospital for treatment to a cut hand.

"The Beatles left the studios at 10.30pm and they escaped the 60 teenagers who reached the entrance gate by travelling in three separate cars which left through the store doors of an old boiler house at the opposite end of the building to that where the youngsters were waiting. By the time they realised what was happening and had sprinted to the other gate, the cars were roaring towards London."

The Beatles in 1965.

On the previous day, The Beatles were greeted by deafening screaming and further hysteria when they flew into Heathrow from their American tour. Guildford teenager Jackie Everett recalled: "There were hundreds of girls on the roof of the terminal and every time there were lights in the sky, they began to scream in anticipation. There were 3,000 girls there and the Beatles waved as they walked across to the limousine waiting right next to the terminal ready to take them to the VIP lounge."

It was nigh impossible for the Beatles to live any form of a normal life with hysterical girls besieging them wherever they went. So they had to stay indoors. Well, nearly always.

By 1968, so many people were dressing like the Beatles – sporting sideburns and moustaches – that it was just a little easier to take a risk.

In the book, The Beatles, by Hunter Davies, John Lennon describes his visit to the Embassy in Esher with Ringo Starr: "I did a trial run with Ringo the other day. We went to see an M and W film in Esher. We chose a matinee, thinking it would be quiet but we forgot the schools were off and it was packed. We did not see the end of the film. We had an ice cream and then left. Nobody bothered us. It was just a practice run."

Beatle's wedding at Epsom

A million hearts were broken at Epsom on 21st January 1966 when Beatle George Harrison married model Miss Pattie Boyd in a seven-minute ceremony.

Complete secrecy was observed and only the immediate families and a few close friends of the bride and bridegroom were told.

A few minutes before 11am, a fleet of cars drew quietly into the foreground of the Epsom Register Office in Ashley Road. The couple hurried in surrounded by relatives.

Miss Boyd, wearing a three quarter length fur coat, white stockings, brown and grey block shoes, carried a posy of flowers. She was hat-less.

It was the only wedding held that morning at the register office. The best man was Mr Brian Epstein, manager of the Beatles. Only Paul McCartney was able to attend from the group. Ringo Starr and John Lennon were both abroad. Harrison was aged 22 on his wedding day. The ceremony was short and simple. It was conducted by Mr Leonard Clarke.

The photo shows the newly-weds leaving Epsom Register Office. Some years later, Pattie Boyd and George Harrison split up and she married rock star Eric Clapton from Ripley, who Harrison sometimes used to call on in his white limousine.

1962: George Street, Croydon, looking towards the town from East Croydon Station. On the right, at number 101, is Rossi Bros. ice cream parlour which also served as a coffee shop. A few doors down is the Utopia florists and at the end of the parade a Croydon landmark, the Thrift clocktower, demolished in the early 1960s. On the left is The Railway Hotel and the turning for the car park. The pub closed in 1962, soon after this photograph was taken.

1969: George Street, Croydon, looking west from East Croydon Station at 3.20pm on Saturday 15th November.

Croydon High Street in 1963, looking towards the corner of Surrey Street and Milletts with Grants dominating the distant skyline.

Vandalism, robbery, a schoolgirl's protest — and arrest of 'The Hooded Phantom'

Croydon in 1966

THE eventful year of 1966 began in controversial mood as big rent increases were announced. Tenants would have to find another 2 shillings to half a crown extra. Croydon's rent officers Mr Butler and Mr Barclay said they had been far from idle in answering inquiries.

It was also a sombre start as it was stated that in 1965, Croydon had experienced its worst ever year for traffic accidents, reflecting a national trend. In Britain, one person in 136 of the population was either killed or injured, a total of 385,499 people.

In the showrooms a Morris Mini Minor could be bought for £450, a new Triumph 1300 for £797 12s 11d or an upmarket Daimler 2.5 litre VA for £1,450.

During **January** it was announced that Croydon's Tory Council Rate Payer's Majority Group would support the maintenance of the 11-plus system. Educa-

tion was to dominate all other news items and a week rarely went by without a mention in the borough's newspapers and particularly the question of comprehensive schooling.

Mid January was very cold with even day temperatures below freezing and nearly 50 girls from Old Palace School walked out of lessons due to Arctic conditions in the classroom. They besieged the *Croydon Advertiser's* offices. It was alleged that the temperature fell to 39F and pupils were not allowed to put their coats on though the headmistress maintained it was 55F to 62F.

On the streets it was icy, too, as rain fell on the 20th January with temperatures well below freezing producing a dangerous glaze. There were scores of accidents with pedestrians receiving broken bones as they slipped and slid to work and some trains took two hours to travel 10 miles to London. Some parking

Work is well under way on the central Croydon flyover in c.1967. Traffic would be taken over the old town.

meters succumbed to the cold and failed to register when 6d was inserted. The NCB advertised that up to seven radiators and all domestic hot water run by a 50,000 B.T.U. boiler, costs just £320.

In the early spring a vigilante squad was set up at Addington to protect telephone boxes from vandalism. It was suggested that the new subscriber trunk dialling system was not as robust as the old Button "A" boxes and did not stand rough treatment.

A series of lectures at Croydon Technical college emphasised the usefulness of computers. "They are now within the scope of most firms in the country but they are no better than the people who use them. Numbers on the course were swelled by staff from Croydon Town Hall as Croydon Council are planning to install a computer," reported the *Croydon Advertiser*.

The rent debate hotted up as 30 people were ejected from council chambers because of numerous interruptions during a meeting on the new rent increases. A crowd some 50 strong jeered council members as they left.

An appointment caused a stir at St Dominic's Church, Waddon. The new priest denied he was in any way connected to the Beatles, a rumour that had raised some excitement amongst the teenagers in the congregation. His name was John Lennon.

An amazing and daring robbery took place at the Stanley Halls, South Norwood Hill. Six 60 lb bronze busts were stolen from their niches 20 feet above ground level. The question was how were they appropriated in an exposed position in full view of two roads?

An appeal was made on television to no avail.

On the **31st March** General Election there was an extraordinary result in Croydon South. There were two re-counts and it was thought the Conservative MP Sir Richard Thompson was the winner but a bundle of 100 votes was found wrongly placed on the Conservative pile and three times escaped detection, eventually spotted by a sharp-eyed labour agent and Labour MP David Winnick triumphed by 81 votes.

After a few spring-like days, a snowstorm swept the borough on the **14th April** and traffic came to a halt on Gravel and Spout Hills. It was warmer in the cinemas where at the ABC Purley or the Regal Purley one could watch "Carry on Cowboy" with Sid James and Kenneth Williams or at the Astoria, Purley "That Riveria Touch" by Morecambe and Wise.

The first few days of **May** were warm and sunny and summer bargains were available at C&A. Ladies' summer dresses sold for 10 shillings (50p), blouses for 7/7 (37p) and swimsuits for 20/- (£1). Also this month, the GPO placed an advert 'We use Computers! But we need you to make them work.' Clerical officers

East Croydon Station, George Street, on Saturday 14th December 1963.

could expect to receive £381 at 16 years rising to £790 over 25 years.

Vandalism continued to hit the headlines and a shopkeeper at Milne Road East, Addington, formulated a plan. He said residents should band together and each night should sit in their gardens behind bushes and await an act of vandalism. Then one should spring out and report the vandals to the police!

There was an outcry after a boy was badly injured in a Croydon street when an abandoned car exploded. Figures revealed that 812 cars were dumped on the borough's roads in 1965.

A report out in **mid July** talked of a proposed M23 motorway which would run from London to Brighton with Hooley and Cane Hill affected in Croydon though it would pass over the Chipstead Valley on a 120-foot viaduct. The motorway would be an eight lane giant, the most costly in Britain. An article in the *Croydon Advertiser* spoke of a projected frightening increase of traffic on the roads by 1981.

A points failure led to a bizarre twist to a journey for 600 rail passengers on the 6.55am Lewes to Victoria service. It became the Lewes to London Bridge train. Due to trouble with a point the train was to be re-routed via Crystal Palace but at Norwood Junction Station the signalman thought it was the Coulsdon to London Bridge Service and it sped on to London Bridge leaving confused station staff at Victoria wondering where their train had vanished to and irate commuters faced with arriving late at their offices.

A two-year-old child was found at home alone in New Addington wearing only a vest. The parents admitted neglect and the little child followed the path of a younger brother and sister and was taken into care.

The contract for the Old Town Flyover was awarded to Higgs and Hill at a cost of £1,375,000. Half a mile long, it was to be an integral link in Croydon's Ring Road. Two months later in September, the cost had escalated to £3,585,000.

From **August** to the year's end, the incinerator at Mayday Hospital was never out of the news. The surrounding area was reported to be carpeted in a black snow-like substance. It was ash which coated cars, washing and paintwork. Residents dared not leave their babies in the garden. A new grit arrester would overcome the problem, a spokesman said.

Plans to reorganise Croydon's secondary schools changed yet again with the proposed six comprehensive schools being reduced to three.

The Labour MP, David Winnick said, "I do wish they would stop playing around and do what the vast majority of local authorities are doing and genuinely go comprehensive". Meanwhile the incinerator continued to belch out black smoke and ash. It was now felt by engineers that a new stack was needed.

Luckily the weather was not too cold during the first half of **October** as it was announced that school heating would not be turned on for several extra days to save fuel bills. The decision was made from the

Some summer bargains at Grants, High Street, Croydon, in 1963.

centrally-heated office of the Croydon Education Committee. The new date would be the 17th and just as well as the temperature dropped several degrees on this day.

A huge blaze in mid-October lit up Croydon's skies in Tamworth Road. Some 100 firemen and 15 appli-

Bourne and Balmer coach station in Dingwall Road, Croydon, pictured at 7.45am on 23rd June 1961.

ances fought the fire for several hours. Three firemen were slightly injured. The heat was so intense that cars had to be removed and residents could not stand outside their homes. Arson was thought to have caused it. A black cloud continued to hang over the Mayday district and it was now thought that a new flue was necessary to the 100-foot chimney!

Wind was in the news during **November** as what was described as a whirlwind struck the centre of Croydon at 5.30pm on the 15th. Pieces of timber rained down from the 22-storey Taberner House which was under construction and hurtled onto cars. One plank crashed through a windscreen and amazingly only slightly injured the driver. Another narrowly missed a police officer in the yard of Croydon Police Station in Mint Lane whilst another pedestrian was injured in Sydenham Road by a scaffolding pole sent crashing to the ground.

Persisent strong winds have plagued shoppers in St George's Walk shopping precinct. Downdraughts caused by the 23 storey office block have forced the need for a cover to be erected over the Centre.

A man known as the "Hooded Phantom" was caught and jailed. He had raped three women and admitted 64 other charges. His crimes were committed all over South London including Croydon and prompted the greatest and most sustained manhunt ever south of the Thames. He was jailed for eight years.

An armed robbery outside St Martin's bank was foiled when raiders who had coshed two employees of a company who had collected wages could not turn off an alarm in a snatched bag.

They panicked and wildly drove their stolen getaway Jaguar causing mayhem on the streets. There was a trail of damaged cars in Sydenham Road, one car was overturned and the bandits then abandoned their vehicle and escaped over the railway line at East Croydon Station. An appeal was made on Police Five TV programme and valuable information was gained.

It was reported that racing cars of a different kind will roar out of Croydon as the Lambretta-Trojan Group expand their sports car production in premises on the Purley Way bringing all assembly work to Croydon from premises in Rye. In 1965 they built 50 sports cars. The year ended in queasy fashion for the staff of the Gas Board at Purley Way, Waddon. Over 70 of the staff had stomach upsets following a Christmas dinner of turkey followed by traditional pudding. For those in better health it was a perfect **Christmas Day**; fine but frosty, just right to walk off the seasonal excesses.

Bouffant hair styles were all the rage in 1967 as 20-year-old Judy Chable of Malden Road, Worcester Park, proves. Much 'back-combing' and lacquer was required to get the desired effect.

Sutton skiffle champs

Skiffle bands were in vogue in the late 1950s and very early part of the 1960s. The Lincoln Boys, pictured here, were the winners of the Surrey Skiffle Championships held at the Granada, Sutton. Left to right are Brian Fairman, then 18, of North Street, Mitcham; Ken Johnson then 17, of Aberconway Road, Morden; compere David Piltch (later known as David 'Diddy' Hamilton); Roger Swan, 17, of Caithness Road, Mitcham, and Peter Hathersay, 21, of Middleton Road, Carshalton. The picture was taken in 1958, but captures the fashions at the turn of the decade.

Luminous pink lipstick worn

Queen Vic, North Cheam

A patron of the Queen Victoria jazz club at North Cheam in the mid 60s was Christine Gore-Edwards of Sutton, who dressed to impress.

"We wore tights and low-heeled shoes to these jazz clubs. We wore loads and loads of eye make-up. Our faces were pale and we had false eyelashes and pink, luminous lip stick and went to parties everywhere. Sometimes we wore mini skirts made out of denim. Our hair was long and straight with no ribbons. The girls drank beer as well as the men. You only drank because it was hot and you were thirsty from all the dancing. It was noisy and smoky in the Queen Vic but completely trouble free. There was never any violence or threats. Some good bands played there."

The popular club was always held on a Sunday.

An aerial view of Purley crossroads in 1961.

Queen Mother — her foot in a surgical shoe — opens Fairfield Halls

Caterham and Purley

THE picture on the left is a bird's eye view of Purley in 1961 and the traffic jams between the Purley Way and Brighton Road were just as bad then.

It may have been that Princess Margaret was caught in the queues when in 1962 she came to visit Woodcote Grove House on the Coulsdon-Carshalton border on 14th February, wearing a fur coat and a kind smile. The home was run by the Friends of the Poor. In the same month, back from Australia, Cliff Richard and the Shadows appeared at the ABC Croydon to launch their Young Ones musical.

In November 1962, Warlingham and Whyteleafe fell out after Warlingham described its neighbour as a 'slummy area' in a dispute over where flats should be built.

Twenty-nine motorists were fined £1 each at Caterham Court for defying parking restrictions in Caterham Valley roads, and if drivers having paid their penalties still had any money left they could walk back to happiness by going to the ABC at Croydon on 11th December to hear Helen Shapiro and Eden Kane. Tickets were from 5/6 (27½p).

It was a glittering occasion on the night of Friday 2nd February 1962 when Croydon's new £1,250,000 Fairfield Halls were opened by the Queen Mother looking 'radiant and happy although handicapped slightly by having to wear a surgical shoe on the foot she fractured some weeks ago', the *Caterham Times* noted.

'Her Majesty was greeted by the Mayor and Mayoress of Croydon, Coun. and Mrs John Aston and the Earl of Munster, Lord Lieutenant. A large crowd waited outside the halls for the Queen Mother. Dame Peggy Ashcroft, the Croydon-born actress, opened the theatre named after her. A huge ice cream gateau shaped as a replica of the halls had been prepared for the special guests.

In Waddon, residents expressed anxiety at ice-cream sellers who sounded their chimes until 9.30 at night and sweet shops which sold young children a chewing gum which 'could be perilous if swallowed'.

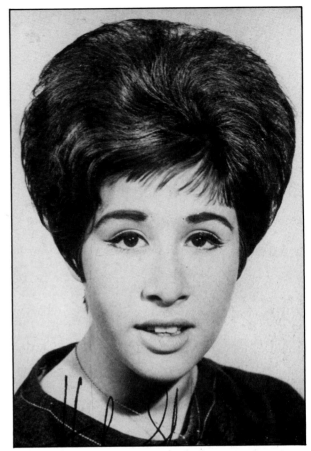

Helen Shapiro who appeared at Croydon ABC in December 1962.

The Orchid Ballroom, Purley – a huge attraction for the young. Nearby residents used to complain about large quantities of scooters parked outside.

At Whyteleafe, councillors were urged to reject plans for an 'American-style' level crossing at Whyteleafe 'with flashing gates'.

On 8th December, a major fire broke out at Grace and Marsh Ltd, building contractors, Purley Way. The smoke must have added to the problems from smog that month. Deaths from pneumonia and bronchitis in Coulsdon and Purley in the foggy spell were four times higher than usual, and double the average in Croydon.

Mayor beat train strike by riding on the back of son's scooter

Life in Wallington, 1962

THE biggest talking points in Wallington in 1962 were the heavy snowfalls at the beginning and end of the year, the miserable summer inbetween, a smallpox scare and the Greater London plan which proposed to take Wallington out of Surrey and into the huge GLC area.

Other topics discussed over the garden fences and at the corner shops were the increased opening hours of pubs, the biggest ever single increase in the rates, the Liberal and Labour gains and the extensive redevelopment of the town.

In 1962, land at Croydon Airport was set to be auctioned. A new courthouse opened, providing magistrates with their first permanent home in over 20 years, and the central library extension plans were put into action. There was also much talk about a London to Brighton motor road route which threatened to slice the borough in two. (This was the proposed M23 extension later abandoned.)

In **January 1962**, following a heavy snowfall on New Year's Eve, the council worked 18 hours a day for a week to clear roads of ice and slush. Council tenants faced 30 per cent rent increases and protests followed. The Labour party and other protestors took round petitions. Wallington's Co-op tried for a licence to sell alcohol but failed. The town's public health

Headlines from the Wallington Times 23rd May 1963.

authorities were besieged with pleas for vaccination after a smallpox scare. The police chased a car loaded with gelignite through the streets at midnight. The car crashed against a tree in Dower Avenue and the occupants appeared in court. The council proposed a shopping parade precinct on the east side of Woodcote Road. The new vicar of Wallington was named as Rev. David Thompson.

February 1962. A rail strike caused "a lot of heartburning and worry" according to the *Wallington Times*. The mayor, Ald. E.P. Vaughan, travelled from the City to a council meeting on the back of his son's motor scooter. Vincyl Products announced that they planned to build a new office block at Butter Hill. Parents of girls at the district's largest private school, Diborben, were shocked to hear from the two headmistresses that the school would probably be closing in the summer when they retired. The parents rallied at an emergency meeting and decided to run it themselves as a Trust.

Residents in **March 1962** complained about cars, motorcycles and scooters parked in roads near the main school. Folk in Woodcote Road, tired of tending to accident victims, launched a campaign for action. Plans to build £5m shopping centre on the Croydon Airport site were turned down. Rates went up to 21s 4d in the pound – a jump of 2s 8d. A timber warehouse belonging to Nursery Furnishings at Hackbridge was burned to the

ground and arson was feared. Traders launched a giant petition to get parking bans removed from Woodcote Road; they were refused. The Minister of Health made a shock announcement to shut the Carshalton, Beddington and Wallington War Memorial Hospital by 1975.

In **May 1962**, the new supermarket on the side of The Odeon Cinema was opened by two chimpanzees. A house in Alington Grove was wrecked by lightning.

July 1962 saw parents angrily demanding why pupils at Park Farm School, Beddington, who had been told by a master they had passed the 11-plus, were further informed they had not. Some of the children, who had been congratulated at a celebration party, "cried bitterly". The annoyance of residents over a power cut turned to shock when they learned the cause – a man had been electrocuted at Beddington power station.

August 1962 saw work begin on the new Jubilee Gardens fronting Stanley Park Road which was to link up with the Town Hall Garden. Plans for a 'super borough' of Wallington-Carshalton-Sutton were announced as originally recommended by the Royal Commission. Work was soon to start on the post office site in Woodcote Road it was stated.

In **September 1962** Mike Sarne announced at Wallington after a one-night show at the public hall that he was leaving showbusiness. He didn't.

October 1962, details of plans to improve Croydon Road, Beddington, with a dual carriageway, roundabout and pedestrian subway were unveiled.

A Beddington man in **November 1962** found a giant mushroom, 33 inches around, growing in his bean row. Beddington and Wallington Council celebrated its silver jubilee.

Stones' first Surrey performance was at Woodstock Hotel

Rolling into North Cheam

ONE of the world's best know rock groups, The Rolling Stones started their career in the dark and dingy backrooms of Surrey pubs in the autumn of 1962.

Although not hailing from Surrey, the Stones soon developed local connections after Brian Jones, the band's founder advertised in *Jazz News*. The first applicant lived in Cheam. He was Ian Stewart who was a brilliant pianist and who remained in the background, out of the limelight, for a large part of the Stones' career. Ian Stewart was the fifth Stone. He lived for many years in a classy home at the top of Banstead Road, Banstead, with his wife, Cynthia, and callers to his home would often include top rock stars. When he split from his wife, he moved to Higher Drive, Banstead. He was the Stones' road manager and best friend. He died aged 47 on 12th December 1985 from a massive heart attack.

A memorial concert in his honour was held in London's 100 Club soon after his death, and the performers included Eric Clapton, Jeff Beck and Glyn Johns.

But back in 1962, the Stones were glad to play in any pub that would have them and put up with their new-style form of blues and their shockingly casual clothes and quite long hair for the time.

The Rolling Stones' first listed Surrey gig was at the Woodstock Hotel, North Cheam, on 5th October 1962 – without Bill Wyman – and it is probable that their first in a series of performances at the Red Lion, Sutton High Street, was in November 1962 – without Bill Wyman or Charlie Watts. But the band, minus Charlie Watts were definitely back at the Red Lion in December and on 9th January. Thereafter, the complete line-up re-visited the venue in 1963 on 23rd January, 6th and 20th February, 6th and 20th March and 3rd and 7th April.

More than thirty years on, the room they used to play in is still there, but is now equipped with a snooker table. The only reminder of those days when they played to just 20 or 30 local fans is a CD juke box which contains the Stones' greatest hits. In 1994, the landlord had heard about the Stones playing there. He had also been told that they were 'booed off stage', but this rumour has probably been embellished over the years.

Don't Be Mislead!
HEAR THE REAL, AUTHENTIC
RHYTHM & BLUES SOUND
. THE .
ROLLING STONES

EVERY THURSDAY	MARQUEE
FRIDAY, 11 JAN.	RICKY TICK WINDSOR
EVERY SATURDAY.	RICHMOND SANDOVER HALL
EVERY MONDAY.	FLAMINGO
FRIDAY, 18 JAN. (EVERY ALT. FRI.)	RED LION SUTTON

GER 6602 or 102, EDITH GROVE LONDON, S.W.10

Advertising the performances at the Red Lion, Sutton, in 1963.

It was in the Red Lion on the cold and foggy night of 5th December 1962 that Bill Wyman first met the future 'fifth Stone' Ian Stewart. Wyman had been invited to watch a live band, The Presidents, by a musician friend, and Stewart was in the audience. In the book, Stone Alone, by Bill Wyman, it is documented that Stewart invited Wyman to a Stones' rehearsal on 7th December 1962. The acceptance of the invitation changed Bill Wyman's life.

Brian Jones had also had a taste of Surrey life. While attending a gig at the Wooden Bridge Hotel, Guildford, in about January 1960, when he was 17, he and a married 23-year-old woman, found they were attracted to each other and had a one-night stand. In February, she realised she was pregnant and a baby girl was born in August 1960, writes Wyman in his book.

Brian forged a link with an important character Giorgio Gomelski in 1962. As a film-maker, Giorgio had recorded the Chris Barber Band at the jazz festival held at the Athletic Ground, Richmond, in

JAZZ

Nowadays it means the music that goes round and around—or the Rollin' Stones are gathering them in

.... is draw....

From the *Richmond and Twickenham Times*, 13th April 1963.

August 1961. This man was by 1963 running his own club in a backroom of the Station Hotel, Richmond, calling it the Crawdaddy after a Bo Diddley song Doing The Crawdaddy. He soon had the Rollin' Stones playing there and their first concert was on Sunday 24th February 1963 in that bitterly cold winter. It was a clear, frosty night after a very crisp winter's day, and in Richmond Park the snow still lay on the ground.

Giorgio had advertised the first Stones concert at Richmond in the Melody Maker, promoting the band as 'R&B with the inimitable, incomparable, exhilarating Rolling Stones'.

Wyman's diary recalls: "The big day went fairly quietly. I met the band in town and we all drove the van to Richmond and set up our equipment. To an audience of about 30, we played two 45-minute sets finishing with a Bo Diddley song called Doing the Crawdaddy. We earned £7.10s. between us."

Promotor Vic Johnson, writes Wyman, remembered that he was "absolutely fascinated by the effect they had on the audience. The kids who seemed pretty biased at first, were galvanised into action. I honestly didn't know whether to laugh at the Stones or send for an animal trainer. I'd never seen anything like them."

Many more gigs were put on by the Stones at Richmond's Crawdaddy Club as well as at the Wooden Bridge Guildford, and Eel Pie Island near Richmond, in the first half of 1963. They played at the Wooden Bridge seven times; Eel Pie Island hotel 18 times and the Station Hotel, Richmond, 13 times before the Crawdaddy Club moved to the Athletic Ground, Richmond, in June 1963. At Guildford Odeon, stiletto heels were dug into fans' shoulders as girls clambered towards the stage. Forty police attended.

Drummer Charles Watts in action, with pianist Ian Stuart in the background, taking a break on the maracas.

Charles Watts and 'Stuart' (Ian Stewart) pictured in the Richmond newspaper article on the early Crawdaddy performances.

The Rolling Stones pictured at one of their earliest concerts at the Crawdaddy Club, Station Hotel, Richmond, probably on 31st March 1963.

Dimly-lit Crawdaddy Club was humble beginning

Stones played to 50 at Richmond

ONE of the teenagers in the audience at the Stones' early performances at the Crawdaddy Club in the Station Hotel, opposite Richmond Station, was William Harvey from Ewell.

He remembered: 'It was dimly lit in there and people were squashed together, but the atmosphere was terrific; there was never any trouble.'

Even the *Richmond and Twickenham Times* – a staid and very traditional local paper got excited. An article in their 13th April 1963 edition carried a full report on the extraordinary scenes that the Stones were causing in their town.

'A musical magnet is drawing the jazz beatniks away from Eel Pie Island, Twickenham, to a new mecca in Richmond. The attraction is the new Craw-Daddy Rhythm and Blues Club at the Station Hotel, Kew Road – the first club of its kind in an area of flourishing modern and traditional jazz haunts.

'Rhythm and blues, gaining more popularity every week, is replacing 'traddypop' all over the country, and even persuading the more sedate modernists to leave their plush clubs. The deep, earthy sound produced at the hotel on Sunday evenings, is typical of the best of rhythm and blues that gives all who hear it an irresistible urge to 'stand up and move'.'

The reviewer, Barry May, described the new form of 'original American Negro pop-music' and noted: 'Modernists and 'traddies' can be seen side by side at the Station Hotel, listening to resident group, the Rollin' Stones.

The modern day Spring at Ewell. The Stones stayed in the upstairs rooms while resting before performances in 1963–4.

The Rolling Stones played at the 3rd National Jazz Festival in Richmond on 11th August 1963.

'From a meagre 50 or so on the club's first night less than two months ago, attendances have rocketed by an average of 50 a week to last Sunday's 320. And the membership book lists more than 700 names of rhythm and blues devotees from all parts of London and West Surrey.

Writing about the young Stones, the *Times* continues: 'Semi-professionals now, although the average age of the group is only 20, the daytime occupations of its members are as varied as the instruments they play.

'The 300 and more in their late teens and early 20s who pack the club on Sunday nights do a dance similar to the craw-daddy. But most improvise on a wildly remote form of the hully-gully, similar to the twist.

'For those less inclined to express their feelings for the music, physically, the Rollin' Stones also provide visual entertainment.

'Hair worn Piltdown-style, brushed forward from the crown like 'The Beatles' pop group – 'we looked like this before they became famous' – the rhythm section, piano, drums and bass guitar provide a warm, steady backing for the blues of the harmonicas and lead guitars.

'Save for the swaying forms of the group on the spotlit stage, the room is in darkness. A patch of light from the entrance doors catches the sweating dancers and those who are slumped on the floor where chairs have not been provided.

'Outside in the bar, the long hair, suede jackets, goucho trousers and Chelsea boots rub shoulders with the Station hotel's regulars, resulting in whispered mocking, though not unfriendly remarks about the 'funny' clothes.'

The Beatles did attend one performance later on and chatted with the Stones in the interval.

Despite demolition threats, the pub survived, and in June 1968 changed its name to the Bull and Bush. In mid 1990s, there was nothing in the pub in the way of souvenirs to remind visitors to Richmond of its dizzy days in the Sixties even though Mick Jagger at this time made his home in the town. Once again, the only reminder was the CD player which offered tracks like Paint it Black and Get Off My Cloud at three goes for a £1 coin.

The Stones also played at Epsom Baths twice in the winter of 1963–4; at Guildford Odeon twice in 1963–4; The Civic Hall, Guildford, in December 1963; Fairfield Halls, Croydon, in December 1963 and 1964, and at Kingston Granada in February 1964. There were additional gigs at Wallington Public Hall in April 1964 and the Ricky Tick Club at the Plaza Ballroom, Guildford, in March 1964. Their last Surrey gig was their second show at the Fairfield Halls on 4th December 1964.

A member of the audience at the Guildford Odeon was Paul Rutterford. He recalled: 'When they did Little Red Rooster, people were standing on the seats. I was still at school. The girls were screaming all the time from the time they came on to the time they left. They played only for three quarters of an hour. I believe Shane Fention and the Fentones were the support.'

A teenaged girl from Abinger, called Viv, at the same concert told her friend, 'I'm going to scream. Scream with me!'

Sometimes when they had to play in Surrey, the Stones would rent a room on the first floor of the Spring hotel at Ewell village. Here, they would unwind, get ready for their performance and sit around playing cards and drinking in the ground floor bar.

1968 murder solved after 33 years

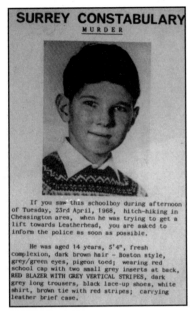

SURREY CONSTABULARY
MURDER

If you saw this schoolboy during afternoon of Tuesday, 23rd April, 1968, hitch-hiking in Chessington area, when he was trying to get a lift towards Leatherhead, you are asked to inform the police as soon as possible.

He was aged 14 years, 5'4", fresh complexion, dark brown hair – Boston style, grey/green eyes, pigeon toed; wearing red school cap with two small grey inserts at back, RED BLAZER WITH GREY VERTICAL STRIPES, dark grey long trousers, black lace-up shoes, white shirt, brown tie with red stripes; carrying leather brief case.

Police appeal after Roy Tutill's murder in 1968.

Killer Brian Field and his first wife, Cecilia Hamilton, who was to die just nine months after her wedding in February 1966.

Murderer Brian Field as a young man in 1957 when he appeared on TV's This Is Your Life hosted by Eammon Andrews. Field's step-father was the main guest.

For 33 years, the murder of Surrey schoolboy Roy Tutill in 1968 remained a mystery. Roy, 14, met his killer after trying to hitch-hike home from Kingston Grammar School to Brockham, near Dorking, on Tuesday April 23rd 1968. He was last seen thumbing a lift at Leatherhead Road, Chessington, after walking from the White Hart, Hook, to which he had caught a 65 bus.

It was thought at the time he had climbed into a silver-grey Austin Westminster Mark Two Saloon. Police traced thousands of vehicles matching the description and eliminated as many drivers.

Roy's body was found dumped in a copse at the Lord Beaverbrook estate, Givons Grove, Leatherhead, three days later. He had been sexually assaulted and strangled.

Police over the years reviewed the case but the culprit was not tracked down until a remarkable development in 2001.

Advances in DNA technology over the years had produced reliable samples for the first time, using original swabs from Roy's body. A chance drink-driving arrest in Solihull led to Brian Lunn-Field, 65, being DNA tested in 2001. The National Crime Faculty matched the result with Field, who in 1972 had tried to abduct a teenage boy in Aberdeenshire and who in 1986 had been jailed for four years for trying to kidnap and assault two teenaged boys in Oswestry.

Field eventually confessed to murdering Roy, using the boy's school tie, and was jailed for life. At the time he was living in Brewery Lane, Byfleet. In 1966, while working for the Milk Marketing Board, Thames Ditton,

Brewery Lane, Byfleet, where the killer lived in 1968 with his second wife, Mary Robinson.

he had married Cecilia Hamilton, 24. She died in a road accident nine months later after fleeing from Field's car in a night-time row on the A3 in Hants after a party in Shepperton. He had been celebrating his appointment as a milking machines engineer at the Milk Marketing Board.

After killing Roy, Field kept the boy's body in the boot of his Mini for three days.

Police never interviewed Field at the time. He moved with his second wife, Mary, to the Midlands within weeks of the murder. They later divorced.

At the time of his arrest three decades later, he was working as a gardener in Solihull.

The long cold spell of 1962-3 made simple shopping trips difficult for housewives and these two in Northcote Road, New Malden. Also pictured is the old BBC receiving station at Tatsfield near Oxted, high on the North Downs.

Big freeze of 1962-3

The coldest winter since 1740

MOST winters have at least a few snowy days. At the end of December 1961 a snowstorm gave over seven inches with deep drifts in places. However it did not last long. The snow that started to fall on Boxing Day afternoon 1962 was looked upon as festive but fleeting.

Ominously next morning it was still snowing. Kerbs had disappeared, paths were buried and many roads became impassable and still it continued to snow with nearly a foot on the Downs. Gatwick Airport near Horley came to a standstill.

However, a worse foe was to follow a few days later on the 29th – a blizzard of fine snow crystals which built up enormous drifts. Nationally 95,000 miles of roads were snowbound and 200 roads completely blocked. A councillor at Walton estimated that 750,000 cubic yards of snow fell on his town. In East Surrey the village of Mugswell was isolated near Reigate Hill and even a snowplough got stuck in nearby Chipstead. Five trains were snowbound at Epsom Downs Station and the A3 at Hindhead was obstructed by billows of snow whipped into grotesque drifts by the fierce east wind. Two doubledecker buses on the Grayswood-Whitehill Service had to be dug out by army personnel.

The main Guildford-Horsley road, A246, was impassable for a time and so was Pebble Hill near Dorking and many byways across the Downs and the sunken lanes through the sandstone ridges south of Albury and Abinger remained blocked for anything other than four-wheel drive vehicles until early March. Some 2,000 tons of salt and 6,000 cubic yards were used by the county's road department in a desperate battle with the elements during the month of January alone.

On the sporting front many fixtures were cancelled and a measure of the severity was illustrated by Sutton Rugby Club who did not play a fixture from 22nd December to 2nd March. Unfortunately when they did resume they lost 18 points to nil to Sidcup.

Conditions were well nigh impossible at Beddlestead high on the North Downs near Oxted where the Graham family was isolated for two weeks and it meant an arduous trek across a sea of snowdrifts for Mr Graham to reach Tatsfield to buy supplies for his young children aged fifteen months and one month.

The New Year gave a hint of a thaw on the 3rd but it was short lived and what followed was the coldest winter since 1740. At Merstham the ground lay under a thick carpet of snow for 66 consecutive days. As the skies cleared overnight on the 23rd January the mercury fell to just 2F[–16.7C] in the Horley-Charlwood area. The long freeze led to some remarkable scenes, none more so than the sight of people sitting in chairs in the middle of the frozen Thames at Shepperton drinking pints of beer. There were reports in the Thursley area of foxes so emboldened by hunger that a bullock was chased into a ditch and torn to pieces and near Felbridge cat-owners were told to keep their pets indoors for fear of being attacked by starved and craven foxes.

The winter of 1962-3 was the coldest since 1740 in Surrey. Heavy snow falls on Boxing Day and again in late December crippled transport. The temperature remained near freezing point until early March. Here, motor cars lay buried in snow at Mogador Road, Lower Kingswood, high on the North Downs near Reigate Hill.

By mid January, the River Thames had frozen over along its Surrey stretch, and people were able to walk across the ice at Chertsey Bridge (above). A mini car was driven over the ice at Kingston Bridge.

Surrey Council Council still ran the fire service at New Malden in 1961.

Surrey loses towns to London

SURREY faced a major shake-up in 1965 after the Royal Commission drew up new boundaries for the county.

Kingston, Croydon and Richmond were swallowed up by the newly-formed Greater London Council and the Surrey boundary line was moved south so that its most northern limits were Staines, Sunbury, Esher, Epsom and Ewell, Banstead, Caterham and Warlingham, Chelsham, Farleigh and Tatsfield.

Surrey said farewell to such well-known councils as Beddington and Wallington Borough; Merton and Morden Urban District; Surbiton Borough; Malden and Coombe Borough; Wimbledon Borough; Sutton and Cheam Borough; Carshalton Urban District; Mitcham Borough, County Borough of Croydon and Kingston upon Thames Borough.

On 8th March 1965, a civic dinner was held at Croydon's Fairfield Halls to mark the end of 76 years as a County Borough. Under the Local Government Act of 1963, it had been decreed that Croydon should become an enlarged London borough, swallowing up Coulsdon and Purley Urban District Council, amid grave concerns and protests from its inhabitants.

In this dramatic change, Croydon lost control of its fire brigade, its ambulance service, refuse and sewerage disposal, motor licencing, some of the main

roads and long term plans for the town. The new London borough – found itself with a population of nearly a third of a million in 1965.

Following the shake-up, the new boroughs were:

Staines Urban District	Guildford RD
Sunbury-on-Thames UD	Guildford Borough
Walton and Weybridge UD	Godalming Borough
Esher UD	Hambledon RD
Epsom and Ewell Borough	Farnham UD
Banstead UD	Haslemere UD
Caterham and Warlingham UD	Frimley and Camberley UD
Godstone Rural District	Bagshot RD
Dorking and Horley RD	Woking UD
Reigate Borough	Chertsey UD
Dorking UD	Egham UD
Leatherhead UD	

Local government kept these boundaries until another massive shake-up in 1974 when many boroughs merged and enlarged into districts such as Tandridge, Elmbridge and Waverley.

Happily, the Post Office still considers that towns like Croydon, Kingston and Sutton are still 'Surrey'.

Surrey's population exploded in the mid to late Sixties, rising from 951,990 in 1966 to 1,002,889 by 1971.

In the same period, most Surrey boroughs saw an increase of population of between 1,000 and 5,000 people. Farnham's went up from 29,040 to 31,248 but Egham's was a more modest 30,140 to 30,609. Guildford's rose from 114,570 to 118,748 across its two districts.

Bridge Road, Godalming, awash after the River Wey burst its banks in September 1968.

Hundreds made homeless as Surrey is submerged

September 1968 – a flood story on every doorstep

THE summers during the 1960s were not noted for their warmth and sunshine and some were downright miserable. By the end of August 1968 the ground was saturated after a generally cool and wet summer. Perhaps September would provide a dry and settled spell? Instead over the weekend of September 14th-15th parts of Surrey had as much as three months' rainfall in just 36 hours. Rivers became raging torrents and burst their banks, bridges were destroyed, valleys became vast lakes and thousands of houses were inundated by the angry, mud-laden waters.

On Saturday 14th, a violent lunchtime storm set the rivers rising and when further storms began around midnight it was not long before the A3 road at Pains Hill was six feet under water. During Sunday, torrential rain kept falling and the River Mole, swollen to half a mile in width, dashed against the 200-year-old Downside Bridge and tore it asunder.

An estimated 1,072 million gallons of water poured through Leatherhead and on towards Esher with 1,200 emergency calls to the Surrey Fire Brigade. The Mole Bridge on the Esher Road was under nine feet

Road narrows – and disappears: The Farncombe end of Catteshall Road, Godalming, in September 1968.

Boats are used to ferry rescuers around Guildford High Street which disappeared under eight feet of water at the low-lying end of the town. A young woman trapped in her flat above the tobacconist actually swam through the swirling waters to fetch in some grocery provisions from a shop on higher ground.

Crowds gather both sides of Guildford town bridge to watch how the normally gentle River Wey turned into a monster – leaving the bottom end of Guildford High Street under eight feet of water and inundating many shops and St Nicholas Church. The church has since put up a brass plaque indicating how high the water reached in September 1968.

of water as dawn broke on the Monday morning and soon the flatlands around Hersham were awash and the Longmoor Estate swamped.

Still warm and dry in their beds, the people of East Molesey slept on but early bowler-hatted commuters left for work clutching rolled umbrellas. They departed behind a slowly unravelling disaster as a wave of water swept under the railway arch on the Molesey Road and those taking the later trains turned and fled as the pavements disappeared under swirling waters in Walton Park. Soon Molesey was to be a district with a flood story on every doorstep.

That evening, those same commuters would return – this time by boat – bewildered, confused and anxious as to what state their homes would be in. They passed smashed shop windows, drowned gardens with fences submerged, furniture and even cars floating in oily black waist-deep waters with people gazing forlornly from upstairs windows.

As the full extent of the flooding became known, a massive rescue and relief plan was put into operation. The army from as far away as Gosport and Aldershot brought three-ton lorries and DUKWS. Sandbags and food were distributed. All police leave was cancelled and to overworked firemen faced with millions of gallons of water to pump away from homes and shopping centres, the task seemed impossible. Ambulance staff set up a series of radio links to overcome breaks in normal channels and then crews often waded waist-deep to reach an emergency.

Help came from all quarters, students, church organisations, WIs, Rotarians, The Red Cross and St John, all assisted at reception centres where hot food and a bed for the night was available – or just a helping hand with the children by reading a story or raising a smile with the odd bar of chocolate.

Over 1,000 people were made homeless in the Hersham area alone. Volunteers took to the boats to

Old Woking High Street in the floods of September 1968. The garage on the left is advertising petrol for 5/9 a gallon (29p) . . . with the added bonus of treble Green Shield stamps.

deliver supplies of milk and bread including well-known TV celebrity Hughie Green, presenter of Double Your Money and Opporunity Knocks. Overall 15,000 loaves and 70 tons of food were distributed.

The flood chaos was not confined to the main rivers. Canoes plied out of Oxted's Fire Station whilst under the railway viaduct only the tops of abandoned cars were seen on the normally busy A25.

Lingfield was entirely isolated whilst at Cranleigh, 400 houses were inundated and 50 people were stranded for the night at the Church Hall. Almost every main road in Surrey was blocked or flooded at some point in the crisis. At Pebble Hill, Betchworth, a landslide of mud, rocks and even trees swept across the road overwhelming a minibus, rolling it over and over and injuring the driver.

Small streams became dangerous torrents and the normally placid Dean Oak Brook in full spate tore away a bridge near Leigh just as a car passed over and swept a lady to her death. A heroic rescue took place in Lonesome Lane, Reigate, as a man dived into the rising waters and brought out first two children and then the driver of a car which toppled into the flood. Seconds later the car was borne away.

As the flood waters went down many people will never forget the overpowering stench of the river water in their homes mixed with the smell of disinfectant that was distributed by council health officials. The sight of piles of rotting vegetables, ruined stock, soaked carpets and twisted furniture that lined every shopping parade and cluttered so many streets and the hum of dehumidifiers would be forever etched in their memory.

Headlines from the Hersham News, 20th September 1968.

'Effeminate' man shocks crowd in smoky club

Marc Bolan's Leatherhead days

A dimly lit club down an alley in Leatherhead lured hundreds of young people to its smoky atmosphere throughout the Sixties.

First called The Chuck Wagon, and then the Bluesette Club from 1966, the venue was a corrugated iron hut at 22a Bridge Street where among the bands who played were John's Children. This group, from the Bookham and Fetcham area, was later joined by Marc Bolan, who went on to form the supergroup T.Rex.

A Fetcham teenager at the time recalled: "When Marc Bolan performed with the band, there was a hot, sweaty atmosphere and everyone was squashed together in there. It was 'new wave' like you'd never heard it before. He had that slightly effeminate touch which was quite shocking at the time, and they were all wearing bright clothes. It was just that bit too much with the make-up, for up until that time, the masculinity of the musicians had been retained from the Fifties.

"I remember this petit chap suddenly appearing with crushed velvet trousers. It was excellent. In a tiny place like Leatherhead, it was quite a thing."

She added: "It was very seedy in there, but there was that lovely smoky, slightly humid atmosphere. It stinked of excitement and gave out that human heat. It hit you bang in the nostrils."

Marc Bolan was Mark Feld before he joined Tyrannosaurus Rex, and he was playing with John's Children when they supported the Who at a very riotous concert in Germany which ended in much violence, smashed windows and punch-ups. Marc had tried to emulate the Who by whipping his guitar with a heavy chain. Mass hysteria broke out soon after and everyone seemed to be fighting.

John's Children consisted of Chris Dawsett, an Epsom Art School student from Fetcham on bass; Geoff McLelland, from Gilmais estate, Bookham, on guitar; Andy Ellison, vocals, and Chris Townson, on drums. John Hewlett later joined. In some combination or another, the band used a variety of names including The Few and The Silence. Andy Ellison developed a stage act of playing the maracas and diving into the audience.

Influential pop manager Simon Napier Bell discovered the band while on holiday in Spain and

Marc Bolan in
November 1965.

**Leatherhead band
John's Children:
Hewlett, Townson,
Ellison and Bolan.**

agreed to see them play as The Silence at the Burford Bridge Hotel, Box Hill. In Who style, Ellison dived into the hotel's swimming pool with his microphone and several amplifiers also ended up submerged. Napier-Bell took this wild band under his wing and got Bolan, who he admired as a songwriter, to join them. He changed their image and got them to dress up in white suits and wear gold medallions. Marc lost interest in the band after the dramatic German tour, and later left. During his time with the band, Bolan is said to have lived near St Mary and St Nicholas Church in Leatherhead. It is rumoured the band's tour van, brought down from Scotland to Bridge Street, Leatherhead, was left in the basement of a construction site by mistake, and is still buried under tons of concrete.

Another exciting venue was the Bookham Youth Centre in Lower Road where Desmond Dekker played despite his fame with The Israelites. The club became a huge attraction for local youth thanks to the efforts of leader John Hyde. DJ Simon Bart also packed the club out.

Leatherhead will also be remembered for The Sky Hi Cafe, bought by the Bluesette owner, Syd Palmer, and the *Chish and Fips* shop in Kingston Road.

In 1963, Leatherhead Urban District Council drew up plans for a one-way system around the town, and stated that the town's bypass was 'under used'. The Crescent Cinema was still showing films and putting on wrestling spectaculars.

food shopping's a pleasure HERE!

AT THE
SUPREME
SUPERMARKET

Open Friday Evenings
TILL
7-30 P.M.

◆◆◆◆◆◆◆◆◆◆

We do not cut just a few items
OVER 500 items cut regularly

◆◆◆◆◆◆◆◆◆◆

Come and see for yourselves
at Cobham Road Fetcham

◆◆◆◆◆◆◆◆◆◆

WE GIVE GREEN SHIELD STAMPS

TAYLORS

1-3 HIGH STREET, LEATHERHEAD   Phone 2431

PEDIGREE ASTRAL

See the 1963 Range of Baby Carriages in Standard or two tone colours

Models by Marmet Pedigree, Royale, Silver Cross, Tansad, Allwin, Swallow etc.

£19.19.0

Small deposit secures and model is stored until required. Pram Mattresses and bags to suit all models

Cots from £3.10.0
Playpens £3.19.6
Playpens with floor £5.19.6
Carry Cots by Enna Luxi products, Slaters, from £10.0
Harringtons
Terry Squares from 37/6
Gauze Squares from 25/6
Cot sheets, Pram sheets and Baby harnesses

Lan-air-cel Blankets Pram and Cot sizes from 15/6
Cot matresses from 39/6

Royale BOSTON

£20.18.6

POLICE CALLED TO DEAL WITH ROWDY TRAVELLERS

Police were called to Leatherhead railway station on Sunday afternoon after a party of two dozen young people had alighted from an Effingham-bound train. They were on the way to Box Hill, but were alleged to have made a nuisance of themselves and smashed light bulbs in the compartments on the journey down.

But, by all accounts, national press reports of the incident

CHUCK WAGON
22A, BRIDGE STREET LEATHERHEAD

FEBRUARY 26th FOLK CONCERT

ROYD RIVERS and GERRY LAUGHRAN

Blues Harmonica and Guitar
Jazz and Folk Club membership 2/6

Lunch and Snacks served daily
(8)

The 'TOP POPS' RECORD & DANCE CLUB
is opening EVERY MONDAY from MARCH 25th
at LITTLE BOOKHAM VILLAGE HALL
7-45 to 10-45   RECORD PRIZES   ADMISSION 2/6   (12)

CRESCENT CINEMA   LEATHERHEAD 3203
SPORTS ENTERPRISES (London) Present
WRESTLING
FRIDAY 18th JANUARY   Commence 8.00 p.m.
£50 A Side Plus Promoter's Purse
MIKE MARINO
Italy. Mid/heavyweight Champion of the World v
Dr DEATH
U.S.A.

Welterweight Contest	Catchweight Contest
ZOLTON BOSCIK Hungary	JOHNNY MAJOR Union of South Africa
v	v
ROGER GREEN Havant	BOB ANTHONY Chelmsford

Middleweight Contest
BERT WATERMAN   v   JOHNNY WILLIAMS
Brixton   Dulwich

Prices: 10/6, 7/6, 5/-, 3/6.   Seats bookable at the Cinema

STRUDWICK SCOOTERS
main agents for
HONDA - LAMBRETTA - CAPRI

Fully-equipped service bay

Spares and accessories

HP and Insurances arranged

Both new and second-hand machines

42 HIGH STREET - LEATHERHEAD
Telephone LEATHERHEAD 3177

The above advertisements and news items taken from the *Leatherhead Advertiser* in the first part of 1963 give an amusing impression of life in and around the town.

Rhythms record shop for the teenagers — Old Wheel tearoom for the ladies

Reigate and Redhill

Reigate High Street on a busy day in 1963.

THANKFULLY Reigate managed to ward off the bulldozers that ran amok in the Sixties, ploughing into anything that stood in their path. Yes, some shops have gone and a number of chain stores have made their home in the town, replacing smaller family concerns, but much of its olde worlde charm has survived.

While the old ladies and those with money enjoyed the tea shops and little eating places, the younger folk used to head for places like The Dive Bar in the basement of the White Hart in Church Street, the Sovereign youth club in Sandcross Lane or the Market Hall at Redhill, where good dances were held and bands like Freddie and the Dreamers and Herman's Hemits played. Some girls would lean over the balcony upstairs and survey the dancers beneath, eyeing up a possible 'catch' for later in the evening.

Other bands who played at the Market Hall included Brian Poole and the Tremeloes while they were at number four in the hit parade with Twist and Shout; Johnny Kid and the Pirates; Swedish group, The Spotnicks and Screaming Lord Sutch who stepped on stage wearing a toilet seat around his head.

The Odeon at Redhill and a youth club in Garlands Road also drew a good attendance. On other nights, small parties would make off to Crawley for ten-pin bowling.

In the late 60s, bands would sometimes play in the upstairs room of the Market Hotel and in about 1969 there was a fight between Earlswood's skinhead gang 'The Brush' and other skinheads.

Youths would amass outside Rhythms record and musical instrument store in Church Street and get up

The foot of Reigate Hill on 1st October 1968. Many of the buildings have since been pulled down and replaced.

to mischief behind the shop premises. Scooters would park outside the shop in the early 60s while their riders went in to browse around the ground floor with its sound booths at the back, or climb the wooden stairs to the television and transistor radio department on the first floor. It was run by a Mr Hurst, a keen snooker player, and there was a similar branch at Redhill. People would come from all around for its large range of sheet music.

Also in Church Street on the same side were other stores including Pauline's ladies's clothes; Robertson's the coffee and high class groceries store which continued for many years run by Mrs E Bates since June 1960; Tesco's; Victoria Wine Co; Elle dress shop, and Irene Skinner hairdressers.

Miss Milbourne, an elderly 'very austere' lady ran the two-storey Old Wheel restaurant and teashop in Church Street. "If you were not good enough in her book, she'd ignore you, and if a Lady came in she would greet her loudly with an enthusiastic 'Good morning'" said one resident. She later died and the restaurant closed. Reigatians still mourn its loss.

On the opposite side of Church Street was Andrew Glass, stationers; the UK Grocery shop; Dainties sweet shop; Gerrard greengrocers; Acres the bakers and Budgens, one of Reigate's first supermarkets.

Redhill remained unaltered throughout the first part of the 1970s, but a huge development programme saw the town change beyond recognition in the 1980s and 1990s.

Redhill High Street.

The Odeon, Redhill, was a popular place of entertainment in 1963.

Ronnie Biggs worked for Reigate Council

Redhill man was a Great Train Robber

Ronald Biggs' visiting card from his Redhill days.

RONALD BIGGS (33). Height 6ft. 1in. Paunchy; dark-brown curly hair. Like Wilson, jail escaper.   BRUCE REYNOLDS (34). Height 6ft. 1in.; fresh, sun-burned complexion; cleft chin

The Sunday Express of 10th April 1966 carries pictures of wanted men Ronald Biggs and Bruce Reynolds, who were partners in crime. After the robbery the two went with holdalls containing £100,000 to Biggs' home at Alpine Road, Redhill.

T HE Great Train Robbery is as much a part of the Sixties as Harold Wilson, the Labour leader, or the Profumo scandal.

Ronald Biggs, at the time of the £2,631,784 raid on a mail train in Buckinghamshire, lived at Alpine Road, Redhill, almost opposite the Holmethorpe Industrial Estate, in a modest semi in a working class area of town.

Born in Lambeth, he became involved in petty crime at a young age and spent a time in Wormwood Scrubs where he met fellow train robber Bruce Reynolds and became close mates.

On leaving jail he took up carpentry and stayed with 'a pretty tough lady' at Merstham, called Ivy, a friend of Reynolds, who, when visiting her, turned up in a 'ritzy sports car'.

In 1958 he worked on Redhill building sites but left for work as a chippie in London. While commuting from Redhill he met 17-year-old Charmian Powell on the train. She was the daughter of the headmaster at Reigate Parish School, London Road, Reigate, and lived with her parents in the school grounds. It was in the classrooms of this school that Biggs and Charmian got involved in amorous activities. They married at Reigate Register Office on 20th February 1960.

Ron was involved in a petty crime spree in the South West in 1958 and was jailed for two years. He was released in time to celebrate the new year of 1960 and Charmian was waiting for him outside Wandsworth. They stayed in a hotel and next day came to Redhill seeking accommodation, while staying with friends John and Violet Goldsmith.

Biggs soon obtained work with Reigate Borough Council as a carpenter. In his autobiography, **Ronald Biggs, Odd Man Out (Bloomsbury 1994)**, he writes of the council job: "Not very well paid but plenty of tea and sympathy with the housewives." He writes that they rented a small flat, planned to get married but Charmian's father was against it.

Ronnie soon changed his job to working for an elderly Redhill building contractor by the name of Sid

Budgeon. He worked overtime because his wife was expecting, and Nicholas Grant Biggs was born on 23rd July 1960 at Redhill County Hospital. "His proud and happy parents wheeled His Nibs through the streets of Redhill in an enormous plum-covered baby carriage."

In April 1962, Ron and Charm had drinks with Charmian's old school pal Janet, and her husband, Ray Stripp, resulting in Ronnie and Ray forming a partnership, Biggs and Stripp, employing ten labourers and operating from the address in Alpine Road.

Ron and Charmian's second son, Christopher Dean, was born on 24th March 1963, putting a strain on the household budget. Ronnie was tempted back to crime when approached by Bruce Reynolds who offered him a £40,000 cut if he were to take part in a job – "enough to buy four new four-bedroomed houses in the best part of Reigate," wrote Ronnie in his book. Biggs knew of an un-named Redhill train driver whose house he was working on in Redhill.

Ronald Biggs and Charmian Powell on the day of their wedding at Reigate Register office on Saturday 20th February 1960.

"While watering plants in his garden, the plan of action was discussed and the train driver agreed to take part", Biggs states.

After the train robbery on Thursday 8th August, 1963, Biggs arrived back home in Alpine Road with Reynolds and they put down two kit bags on the kitchen floor which Charmian learned were full of cash. While he had been away, his brother Jack, had died of a heart attack and the police were looking for him on "a tree felling job in Wiltshire". Next morning the money was tipped on to the bedroom floor. £40,000 of blue five pound notes were in one suitcase and £60,000 in mixed notes in another and more in a holdall. Minders later looked after the proceeds. Ronnie celebrated with an Indian meal in Soho and some window shopping. A pick-up truck later removed £60,000 from the house. Some £40,000 was later taken unwittingly by a cab driver to Horley and handed to another minder at a pub. Both minders received £5,000. Then, back for a celebratory drink in Redhill, Biggs noted the bar girl checking the numbers of notes to make sure they were not from the robbery!

Some days later, one of the robbers was arrested in Bournemouth. And then £100,000 from the raid was found in Redlands Wood, at Coldharbour, Dorking

TRAIN RAID FINDS IN DORKING AREA

Box Hill caravan used by some of the gang?

FOR SOME TIME after the great train robbery, Dorking was the centre of operations for some members of the g ang. This is now clear, following the discovery of more than £100,000 in banknotes dumped in woodland at Coldharbour, and the search this week of a caravan on a site at Box Hill which revealed a further £30,000 in £5 notes which had been hidden inside the caravan.

The money was counted at Dorking police station by the manager of the Midland Bank, Dorking, Mr E. D. Ford, and Mr A. H. Boswell, also from the Midland Bank.

Scotland Yard now believe | soon after the £100,900 was | Among the things inside the they know the names of the | found at Coldharbour on Fri- | caravan were children's toys,

Headlines from the _Dorking Advertiser_ after Great Train Robbery cash was discovered at Coldharbour. The finder raised the alarm by waving down passing motorists Mr and Mrs William Howard of Weald View Cottages, Coldharbour.

by Mr John Ahern whose motor cycle had overheated a few yards away from the trees. He thought someone had left the remains of a picnic, investigated, and unzipping a holdall, discovered it stuffed with £1 notes. Police were on the trail. A further £30,000 cash was discovered in a caravan at the Clovelly site, Box Hill near Headley, concealed behind panelling. This was James White's hideaway. The Chief Constable of Surrey attended the raid on the caravan which had red checked curtains, and was recently vacated by a young pair with a white toy poodle.

Police also raided a retail outlet at Molesey near Hampton Court and made arrests in connection with the inquiry.

The rest is history. Biggs was arrested at Alpine Road, Redhill, by officers including young Sgt Jack Slipper – later Detective Superintendent Jack Slipper. He and colleagues had ripped up his floorboards in the hunt for cash. Some of the proceeds of the robbery had been put in the kitchen stove fire and the ashes scattered on the rosebeds in the garden. The unnamed Redhill train driver was never caught but Slipper years later told Biggs that inquiries had been made amongst railway staff. Three members of the gang remain undetected.

Biggs escaped from Wandsworth jail on 8th July 1965, little over a year into his 30 year jail term for his part in the robbery. He was chased all over the globe by detectives, but eventually enjoyed many years of freedom in Brazil where he had a native son which prevented his extradition. Charmian moved to Australia. Her father tragically took his own life in the Castle Grounds, Reigate, in the mid 70s.

Hopefuls in the Headline Girl contest pictured on 24th July 1967.

The winners

1967

1st	Mrs Joy Willison (25) of Mulgrave Road, Sutton.
2nd	Jacqueline Lodge (16) of Vicarage Lane, Horley.
3rd	Mrs Janet Rowswell (23) of Tynedale Road, Strood Green, Betchworth.

1968

1st	Anne Whyatt (25) of St Paul's Road, Dorking.
2nd	Sara Clark (19) of Belmont Rise, Cheam.
3rd	Margaret Kellingley (21) of Richland Avenue, Coulsdon.

1969

1st	Elizabeth Lokhandvala (20) of Pound Hill, Crawley.
2nd	Tina Hunter (19) of Tynedale Road, Strood Green, Betchworth.
3rd	Dianne Mansell (20) of Horley (Horley's Carnival Queen in 1967).

Competition for 'gaiety, quick wittedness and attractive appearance'

Headline Girl Contest 1967

Girls from Redhill, Reigate, Dorking, Oxted and Horley, were urged in the summer of 1967 to enter a contest. It was allegedly not a beauty competition but one where the judges were looking for star qualities in young women.

One judge, Pamela Farrell, said at the time: "When helping to choose the Headline Girl, I shall be looking out for a young woman who will not merely make the headlines once – but one who will stay there. This I'm afraid, may mean that I rule out the prettiest girl who enters, if all she had to offer are her looks.

"Equally, the girl with the brightest personality won't get my vote if she fails to make the best of

her appearance. A true Headline Girl – a girl with those extra qualities which make news – must, in my view, possess a combination of originality, poise, quick wittedness, gaiety, an attractive appearance, and, on top of that, an extra something which show business people called 'star quality'.

"Although I haven't included beauty as one of the things I'm looking for – I'm much more impressed by good grooming – I must admit that a pretty face will be no handicap."

The contest, organised by Irwin Ferry and Jack Underwood, from the Surrey Mirror and Dorking Advertiser series promotion department at Redhill, offered glittering prizes including a 10-day holiday in Holland travelling on a BUA One-Eleven jet – plus hairstyling at Barry Woolf's in Reigate and a first class trip to be entertained by Norman Wisdom at Torquay. The finals were held at Burford Bridge Hotel, Boxhill, Dorking, on 14th August 1967.

The three pictures above show a promotion at Redhill Odeon on the launch of the box office hit film The Graduate on 27th October 1968.

Headline girls made a guest appearance at the finals of the Miss East Surrey Lentheric perfume beauty contest organised by the Surrey Mirror newspaper of Redhill, and held at the Gatwick Manor Hotel, near Horley, in September 1969.

Some of the contestants for the Headline Girl contest in 1968. A sales representative is covered in suds after demonstrating the Morny beauty bath product in an outdoor tub at the Gatwick Manor Hotel.

Actor Richard Briers – future star of TV's The Good Life – makes a special visit to a party for the 1968 Headline Girls at Gatwick Manor Hotel, near Horley. The cake also refers to the Thorndike Theatre Appeal of the same year at Leatherhead. Briers accepted a cheque from Jack Underwood, from the Surrey Mirror Series promotion team on behalf of the appeal.

Redhill Football Ground and stadium with the Colman Institute and library in the foreground. Both these were to be demolished and relocated a few years after this photograph was taken in 1969.

The Warwick Hotel, Redhill, in 1969, which later faced the bulldozer so that Safeway could be built. The latter ceased trading at the site in the autumn of 1994.

Baby miraculously survived 1969 disaster

Horley air crash killed 50

HORLEY was plunged into chaos on January 5th 1969 when a Boeing 727 crashed killing 50 people.

The Ariana Airlines jet ploughed into a detached house at Fernhill, between the Coppingham Arms, and Shipley Bridge, in thick fog. Visibility was down to just 100 yards at the time.

More than 30 ambulances came from all over Surrey and Sussex, some from as far away as the London Metropolitan area. Sixteen fire engines from the Redhill division and a special appliance designed to deal with air crashes was rushed to Horley from Rye in Sussex.

Over 100 police were summoned and many off-duty men helped cordon off the area and sift through the wreckage. The Balcombe Road was closed to normal traffic so that the injured could be ferried to hospital by relays of ambulances. The plane came down just a few hundred yards from Gatwick Airport where it was attempting to land.

Local organisations were also at the scene of the disaster and the St John Hall in Massetts Road was turned into a temporary mortuary.

More than 60 men from the Horley and Gatwick Divisions of the Brigade staffed the hall and helped provide refreshment and shelter for relatives of crash victims.

Reinforcements were drafted in from Crawley, Redhill, Reigate, Godstone and Caterham Divisions as they worked throughout the night.

Rescuers had to carry bodies across a field, pass them through a hedge and over a ditch. A shuttle system was set up with police and firemen who loaded the ambulances.

One of the survivors was a 16-month old baby girl who lived at the house called Longfield with her parents. Bill and Anne Jones were thought to have been killed instantly when the plane careered into their home at around 2.35am. But little Beverley was saved by the wooden framework of her cot which folded up like matchwood on top of her to form a protection from the flying rubble and twisted metal.

Her cries from the wreckage were heard by 24-year-old PC Keith Symmonds from Oxshott, who was

Flashback to the front page of the Horley Advertiser of 10th January 1969. The picture in the top right hand corner shows miracle baby, Beverley. Her parents, who were killed in the crash, are pictured on their wedding day.

among the first to arrive. He said at the time: "I just could not believe that anyone could possibly have been in that house and survived. Then I heard the crying and looked more carefully at the wreckage and saw a tiny hand waving from a mound of bricks.

"She was bleeding and crying but seemed to have only cuts to her face. I dug the bricks away, snatched her out and rushed her away to the first ambulance."

The miracle child left Redhill Hospital a few days later to start a new life with her grandparents, Harry and Hettie Simmonds, in Crawley.

Bill Jones was the principal of one of the biggest insurance brokers in Crawley at the time. His wife was involved in a bad motor accident just before Beverley was born. She was thrown through the windscreen of a car in a collision. Ann recovered and Beverley was not affected.

An inquiry into the crash said the crew seemed to be searching for aerodrome lights at fog-bound Gatwick rather than relying on their instruments.

Stately perambulators were only traffic hazard

Personal service at Horley's shops

Horley carnival 19th July 1964.

THE expansion of Horley from the pre-Gatwick sleepy town to the not-quite-so torpid town of today was well under way by the early 1960s. Yet at that earlier time, Horley had a feeling of homeliness that modern development has to some extent destroyed.

Never a pretty town in the architectural sense, it nevertheless had, and still has to some extent, a feeling of 'home town' rather than a drifting extension of a larger unit.

The High Street in 1960 exemplified the character of the whole town. Woolworth's had the smell that was unique to the old-fashioned version of the store with its wooden floors and ice cream counter just inside the door. All the counters were individually manned by a saleslady; a feature shared by the town's leading grocer's, Stapley's.

Stapley's – one of three shops run by the same family in the town – supplied all the needs for grocery items that could in later years only be obtained from a supermarket.

Customers were treated as individuals and many were known by name. The shop had a sprinkling of wooden chairs for the weary shopper and goods were weighed on brass balances. Even some of the butter was held in bulk and the required amount was patted into shape and individually wrapped.

At the crossroads were Cross and Herbert's, the chemists; the Gas Showroom; an estate agents and Cooper's, the greengrocers which spilt out its wares in front of the shop under a canvas awning. The greengrocers still hung bananas in large bunches from meat hooks attached to the awning's supporting struts. They also served a secondary purpose – to hang by his walking harness, a customer's small child who otherwise insisted on squeezing the soft fruit.

A few doors away was Mr Bunkell, the fishmonger, who was never without the traditional headgear of a black homburg.

Batchellor's store – later Collingwood Batchellor – performed the same role in 1960 and perhaps is one of the few stores, and possibly the only one of any size, that still retained for decades after the 60s its assistant-to-shopper relationship.

On the other side of the railway track, do-it-yourself enthusiasts frequented Young's store. If they didn't have it, you couldn't get it – at least in Horley.

Back in the town, two cafes, the Green Lantern and Cafe Collette were the base for local gossip for tired shoppers and in the evenings, the entertainment hot spot was the Regent Cinema with two different programmes a week and an old re-release on Sundays.

That apart, the public house served the population for their nightly entertainment, more across the whole age range rather than later when pubs tended to be more the haunt of younger men and women. The forerunner of the Game Bird, The Thorns Hotel, was a well-known stopping place for omnibuses en route between London and Brighton being sited conveniently at the thirstiest point along the route. It was a noisy place then.

Another popular hostelry was the Chequers Hotel. In the early 1960s, the famous old tree in front of the building was then still struggling for life and the hollowed-out trunk was the home of a tramp who may have been short of food but never drink thanks to the generosity of the customers. He claimed, perhaps with some validity, that the site was common land.

In the High Street, there were no yellow lines, car parks or parking problems. The only snarl-ups were on the pavements – caused by many young parents pushing stately perambulators. No-one thought to take their baby inside the store with them in those days.

There were some odd characters, however. One, known as Wurzel Gummidge, worked as a one-man sub-contractor on a housing estate. Despite his body being parallel with the ground, he put many fit men to shame. He was well known for offering building materials to people at extraordinary low prices. Old Tom was another. In hot weather he could be seen, stripped to the waist, propping up his enormous pot belly on the handlebars.

At Chaldon

Signs of the times

In Sutton

Park Hill, Carshalton.

At Ditton Road, Tolworth.

A217, Belmont.

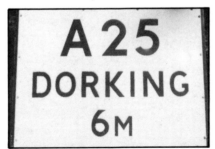

Motoring at Gomshall.

Ditton Hill Post Office.

Near Rough Rew, Dorking.

Brighton Road, Surbiton.

In 1994, all these signs had still survived since the Sixties.

Cobham centre with Fine Fare on the right and Woolworth on the left, c.1963.

The Savoy, Street Cobham, in 1963, showing the Longest Day – a film about D Day. It was pulled down soon after and a parade of shops was built on the site.

The Queen Mother at the Gallaher Gold Cup event at Sandown racecourse, Esher, November 1964.

The Ministry of Labour in Esher, 1963, with Hunter, Dunn and Hollens Ltd, upholstery store next door.

Esher, Cobham and The Dittons

The Ministry of Labour at Esher was visited by those few on the dole during a time when there was much work around. Staff would hand jobless callers a 'vacancy card' to pursue. A week's dole money was around £2. 10s. If nothing was on offer, lads would walk over to the Embassy and see films like 'Blow Up' featuring David Hemmings. Dole cash was handed out through a little window.

Housewives in Long Ditton enjoyed a home de-livery service of milk and groceries by the RACS and the United Dairies.

Streetwise teenagers in the Dittons snubbed short-back-and-sides hairdressers and sought out Andre of Thorkhill Road, Thames Ditton. Schoolboys packed the salon to have Brylcreem-styled cuts with 'Beatles' fringes – risking the wrath of headmasters next day. Sometimes, young lads would queue in the street so great was the demand. A lurid neon sign, filled the tiny window advertising contraceptives. Hair cuts

A children's playground at Sandown was officially opened on 12th July 1963.

were half a crown (12½p). On receiving the money, Tony, the stylist, would reply: "Swinging!" in true Sixties-style.

Youngsters found the Thames Hotel, Hampton Court an exciting place to visit, with Chris Barber and Kenny Ball playing at the regular jazz nights.

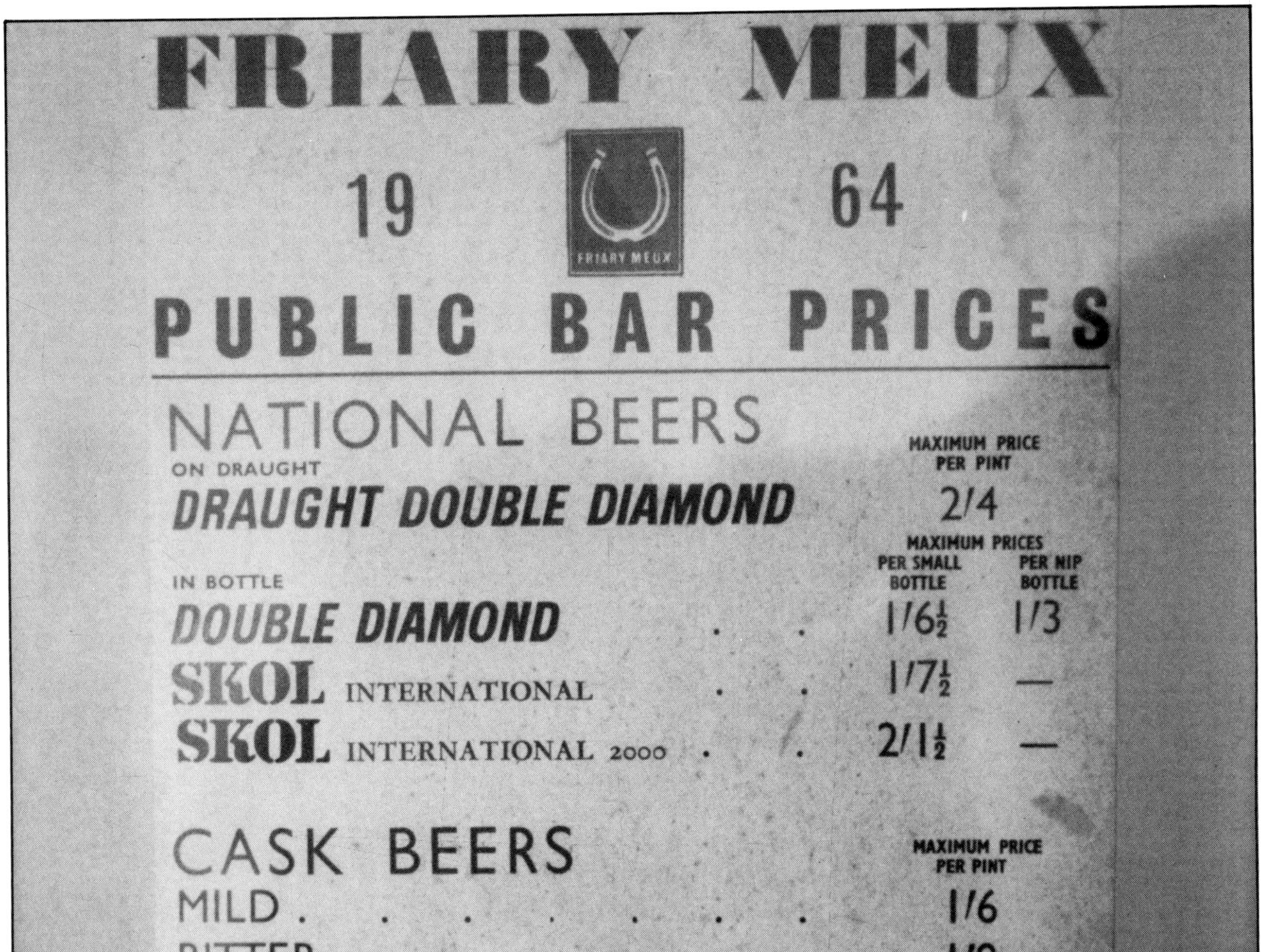

FRIARY MEUX

19 64

FRIARY MEUX

PUBLIC BAR PRICES

NATIONAL BEERS

ON DRAUGHT

	MAXIMUM PRICE PER PINT
DRAUGHT DOUBLE DIAMOND	2/4

IN BOTTLE

	MAXIMUM PRICES PER SMALL BOTTLE	PER NIP BOTTLE
DOUBLE DIAMOND	1/6½	1/3
SKOL INTERNATIONAL	1/7½	—
SKOL INTERNATIONAL 2000	2/1½	—

CASK BEERS

	MAXIMUM PRICE PER PINT
MILD	1/6
BITTER	1/9
'Treble Gold'	2/1

BOTTLED BEERS

	PER LARGE BOTTLE	MAXIMUM PRICES PER SMALL BOTTLE	PER NIP BOTTLE
FRIARY ALE . BROWN ALE	2/3	1/2	—
NIGHT CAP STOUT	—	1/3	—
XXXX	—	1/4	—
'Treble Gold'	—	1/5	1/1½
JUBILEE STOUT	—	1/7	—
MACKESON STOUT	—	1/8	—
ARCTIC BARLEY WINE	—	—	1/10

Sadly, this poster is no longer current, even though it still hangs in the Panther public house at Doods Road, Reigate. A pint of mild is 1s 6d (7p); bitter is 1s 9d (9p) and draught Double Diamond is no more than 2s 4d (12p) a pint.

The shopping parade, Frimley, which housed the Home and Colonial; Gerrards greengrocers; Martin's, a chemist, Milward's and other stores. Watney's White Hart Hotel was on the left, where on winter days like this one, two fireplaces in the large, saloon bar, kept out the cold. Also in the foreground a garage is advertising car batteries from £2.10s.

Peter Sellers and Britt Ekland lived at Elstead

Farnham jives to the jukebox

THE Jolly Farmer public house in Bridge Square, Farnham, was one of the first to install a jukebox in the town. It would have contained all the major hits of 1965 on 45rpm vinyl singles. As the arm of the record selector mechanically clasped the discs and lay them on the turntable, the needle would have undoubtedly picked up the sounds of the year's number ones which included I Feel Fine by the Beatles, Little Red Rooster by the Rolling Stones; Yeh Yeh by Georgie Fame; The Moody Blues' Go Now; You've Lost that Lovin' Feelin' by the Righteous Brothers and Tired of Waiting For You by the Kinks.

The olde worlde pub, dating back to the early 1770s, was actually go-ahead and modern in its way of thinking, for light pub lunches were on offer with well-cooked English food served at the bar or at tables. Some pubs in the area were only beginning to think about serving sandwiches. The Jolly was a Courage pub, unlike the Wheatsheaf in West Street whose brewer was Watney.

At the Wheatsheaf, light lunches including steak,

kidney and mushroom pie were being offered at lunchtimes and on weekday evenings by the mid 60s.

For those who wished to leave their car at home, the pub could be reached by buses 6, 7 and 14 from Aldershot.

And talking of cars, Paul Burch's Natalie Service Station in East Street, Farnham, had a variety of second hand motors on offer in August 1960 at reasonable prices. A 1958 Austin A.35 (off-white, with a heater) was advertised for £425; a 1955 Ford Zephyr Coupe (black with heater) was marked at £400 and a 1956 blue Ford Consul had a £425 asking price.

Picturesque Elstead was home for Peter Sellers, the comedy actor and his second wife, Britt Ekland. They married at Guildford Registry Office on 19th February 1964 and lived in a beautiful mansion with spacious gardens.

A meeting place in Wrecclesham was the Bear and Ragged Staff where the landlord was "a charming Irishman" in the mid 60s.

Camberley, Frimley, Lightwater, Blackwater, Bagshot

Camberley Kate and her dogs

CAMBERLEY's most colourful character was Camberley Kate. She could always be seen around the town, together with her fourteen or more dogs.

She picked up waifs and strays of the canine world and became their loyal leader and provider. Her dwelling was a cottage near Blackwater Bridge which was over-run with dogs and the odd cat.

Almost daily she would set off for her trip into the town with her push cart in which were two or more dogs; the smaller ones at the top. The others were on leads. The assembly would patrol rigorously up the main road, halting motor vehicles in their path until the shopping area was reached. People would stop and chat or place coins in a tin attached to the cart. She didn't like photos being taken and asked those wishing to secure a pictorial souvenir to purchase one of her black and white prints.

One town pensioner, with a smiling face, recalled years later: "She was a queer old bird. When she was coming down the road, traffic had to get out of her way. She used to clean shops on a Wednesday afternoon and tie one or two of these dogs up to the nearest lamp-post to the shop she was working in, and the other dogs would sit there patiently for up to two hours as good as gold before she led them off on her patrol." If any dog didn't fall in line, she would bang the side of the cart with a stick.

Sean Bell, an altar boy at St Tarcisius Church, who served at a pre-funeral memorial service after Kate Ward died in August 1979 aged 84, remembered: "I never saw her standing around gossiping, but kids used to play with the dogs when she stopped. People were not worried about rabies or anything in those days."

The town of Camberley underwent huge changes in the 1960s. In his book, The Story of Camberley, George Wellard writes that just prior to 1960, the population was already 25,000 and fast-growing. The little town consisting of a modest number of shops in High Street, London Road and Park Road, was about to be changed beyond recognition, and so were the central rows of Victorian cottages in Park Street, Princess Street and Obelisk Street. The shops were

Camberley Kate in the Sixties.

then family-run concerns with 'cheery, welcoming shopkeepers who knew their customers by name'.

The Holmdale estate and Hillside's cricket ground had been acquired by the council for a 150-space car park by 1960 and early that year architects were to draw up major plans for the whole shopping centre. In May 1960, their scheme was unveiled at a public meeting held at Agincourt Hall, Yorktown (the industrial estate where 60 firms were by now operating). A multi-storey was envisaged near the railway and the Obelisk Street car park was removed to make way for new shops.

By 1961, the population had risen to 28,552. In 1962, the final plan appeared, and amid grave concerns from townsfolk, the cottages, school, car park and a couple of shops were demolished and the present concrete shopping centre erected in its place. Scores of cottages were bulldozed plus the schools in School Lane and Obelisk Street. The M3 construction started in the same year near Lightwater and Bagshot and continued until 1972 when the Camberley section was opened. Johnson's factory at Frimley was built near the Blackwater River in 1965. In the late 60s, the Warren and Watchetts estates were completed in the main. Many private estates sprung up near the M3.

By the end of the 60s, the population had soared to in excess of 42,000.

The 448 bus service between Guildford and Peaslake or Ewhurst, was operated using these much-loved Guy GS buses in 1963-4. One of them is pictured at Onslow Street bus station, Guildford.

Twist competitions, and Surrey's Loco-Motion Queen were some of the attractions at this Cranleigh beat music show in the icy February of 1963.

Speciality drink at the Cranley Hotel, 1965

A 'warm and cheering' feeling in Cranleigh's pubs

IF you ask a local the way to the Cranley Hotel, you might get a puzzled look, wrote author Richard Keeble in 1965. "If this happens, inquire for 'The Railway' and you will soon be put to right.

"To make it even more complicated, the sign of the house is of a crane bird. It comes from the old name of the village, Cranley. This was changed because of confusion with Crawley.

Keeble's book, Surrey Pubs, states that the hotel which is residential, is near the famous cricket ground on which have played such famous people as Hutton and May.

In winter, a drink certain "to give you a warm and cheering feeling after only a couple" is a Cranley speciality, Wisniowska, a Polish cherry vodka.

Keeble adds: "Ham or cheese are provided with fresh, crispy rolls delivered daily." The public house was a Courage outlet and if you felt it was best not to drive, it could be reached by either the 33 bus from Horsham to Guildford or the number 23, (Ewhurst to Guildford).

Another Cranleigh pub, the Three Horsehoes had Alton Bitter and Watney's Red Barrel on tap.

In the nearby village of Ellens Green, pub goers were greeted in a different way – by "wildly welcoming poodles and the rather fierce-looking German wolfhound (docile really)".

Menus were very limited in the 60s and not all pubs offered lunchtime food. But in the Wheatsheaf you could sample "the excellent home-made soup, cockles, mussels and whelks from enormous jars, or chicken portions from 3s, eaten in 'Henry VIII' style. And these come from local chickens which until their sudden demise had run on open ranges".

Keeble continues: "It is a help-yourself snack bar; the landlord being trusting enough (he was a policeman) to allow the customers to tell him what they had afterwards."

The Parrot at Forest Green also offered a warm welcome with its "enormous log fires of the rambling inn".

At the Windmill Inn, Ewhurst, in 1965, food included "Scotch eggs and sometimes vol au vents. And for a drink with a 'kick' try the landlord's speciality – a 'Whizzo' of which the base is orange curacao."

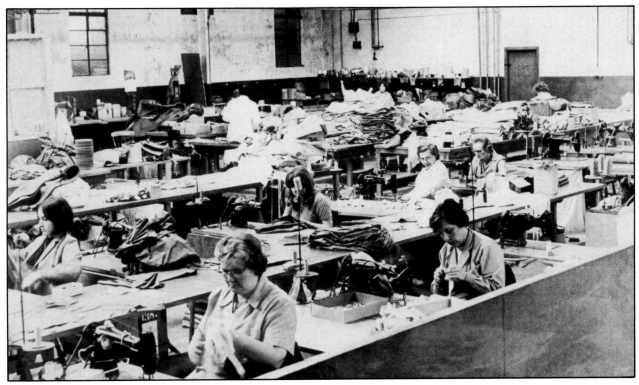

The RFD factory in Catteshall Lane, Godalming, in the early Sixties. The firm made parachutes, inflatable dinghies and lifejackets. The factory later closed but an office remained in Holloway Hill.

Godalming, Witley, Hascombe, Tilford, Loxhill

Good times at Godalming

THE quaint town of Godalming hardly seems the place where big Sixties' bands would come to play, but in its heyday, The Gin Mill Club at the Angel Hotel attracted top acts.

"Anyone who was big in the late Sixties or the early Seventies played there," a former patron, Paul Rutterford recalled some 25 years later. "It was a very small sweat shop and usually packed out." He said that the rock bands Free, Cream and Fleetwood Mac performed there as well as the Chicken Shack group. The hotel was pulled down some years later and shops built in its place.

Outside the town, a more relaxing place to unwind was the White Hart Hotel at Witley where, "As well as the normal selection of alcoholic liquor, there is a particularly good selection of fruit juices, which is explained by the fact that a mile down the road is Enton Hall, where many a business tycoon and theatrical agent adjourn from time to time to lose weight or for general irrigation purposes . . . 'They rarely cheat when they come in here,' says the landlord, 'although they will have an occasional glass of champagne.'"

Another local drive in the motor may have been to The Donkey at Tilford, described as an absolute paradise for children. As well as a playground containing a chute, swing, and roundabout, there was a donkey, monkey, squirrels, a mynah bird and many foreign birds.

"While you are in the bar or sitting on the terrace overlooking the playground, you can be sure that your children are not suffering from boredom."

A local newspaper advertisement for Jordan's Garage in August 1960.

He added: "The present donkey drinks a pint of beer in the bar, but will not go near the ring in the wall to which donkeys used to be tied. 'Reckon he can see the ghosts of his ancestors,' said the landlord."

Lunchtime bar snacks included sandwiches, Cornish pasties and hot sausages, and drinks included Tequila, the Mexican spirit and Danish Snaps.

Nearer home in 1963, the Odeon at Godalming was showing Billy Budd starring Robert Ryan and Peter Ustinov.

Teenagers caused problems, then, like they do today. Hooligans at Milford and Witley left "a trail of damage and senseless mischief" in **January 1963** according to the *Surrey Advertiser*.

Loxhill sub post office near Godalming closed in 1962, disappointing members of Hascombe Parish Council.

During the 1963-3 freeze-up, Hula girls in bikini tops and grass skirts warmed the gentlemen's blood

when they put on a show at Chichester Hall, Witley. At Godalming County Grammar School, old desks were burnt to feed school boilers as the snow stopped coal supplies.

At a social evening in early **March 1963** at Godalming Borough Hall, Godalming, beauties were "out in force, competing for the title of Godalming Co-operative Queen," reported the *Advertiser*. Valerie Stevens (15) from Hascombe came first; Janet Goodship (16) from Witley, second and Wendy Tapp (18) from Elstead, third.

In April 1963, there was nearly a riot at a Godalming girls home, led by a 15-year-old. Windows were smashed and some girls barricaded themselves inside a caravan.

In the town, there were plans to merge the Godalming Co-op and the Royal Arsenal.

Plans were also drawn up in April 1963 to build a £50,000 swimming pool at Broadwater, but there was bad news to follow when it was announced that the Godalming factory, Martin Goacher and Co Ltd in Catteshall Lane was to close with many job losses. The firm employed 55 and manufactured reinforced plastic for the aviation, guided weapon, electronics and radar industries.

Technicolour rain fell from skies

June 1968 was not the most pleasant of summer months with much cloud and rain but it ended on a blazing note with a very fine Sunday just right for village cricket or washing the car.

A few days earlier there had been a series of dust storms over the Sahara and fine sand was swept into the air and carried aloft several miles. Winds were southerly over Europe and it was transported northwards towards Britain.

On Monday morning 1st July people opened their doors ready to go to work and found their vehicles covered in blobs of orange, yellow, red and brown. From Guildford to Oxted light rain overnight falling from the castellated streaked clouds had washed the desert sands and clays from the skies but it had not been enough to rinse it away and thus left the technicolour blotches or untidy smears.

It was estimated that several thousand tons of the Sahara had fallen on Surrey and adjoining counties.

Chertsey's shops in 1966

Victor Value at 77-79 Guildford Street, Chertsey, offered fabulous bargains AND double pink stamps on Tuesdays. Parazone bleach was 1/1½ (5½p); T-shirts were just 2/3 (11p) and polythene bread bins 15/6 (77p).

The Maypole supermarket at 95-99 Guildford Street. Family size tins of peaches were 2s (10p) and roasting chickens 3/2 (16p) a pound.

Woolworth's at 92 Guildford Street. Food is displayed in the window. Lassie dog food is on offer at 1/5 (7p).

Gay's Fashions were at 81-83 Guildford Street, Chertsey.

The London cafe was at 14 Guildford Street near Station Road.

Boots at 88 Guildford Street.

In memory of Kennedy

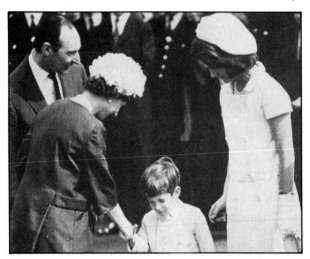

The Queen shaking hands with John Kennedy jnr, 4, as Mrs Jacqueline Kennedy, widow of the President, and Lord Harlech look on at the ceremony in Runnymede, Surrey, on a warm, spring day in May 1965.

SURREY people, like those all over the world, were stunned to hear the announcement of American President John F. Kennedy's assassination on 22nd November 1963.

It was with the full agreement of all political parties in the House of Commons on 5th December 1963 that an appropriate British Memorial to President Kennedy was to be installed in Britain and it was finally decided to erect a memorial at Runnymede near Egham, and donate an acre of land at the same site to the United States. It was at Runnymede that the ideal of human rights was born with the signing of the Magna Carta in the early 13th century.

To complete the memorial, it was proposed that scholarships should be established for young men and women from the United Kingdom to go to Harvard University, Radcliffe College or the Massachusetts Institute of Technology.

A Kennedy Memorial Trust was formed, and the John F. Kennedy Bill, transferring the land to the United States of America, passed all stages in the House of Commons and received the Royal Assent in July 1964.

In a shed at Runnymede, sculptor Alan Collins inscribed the seven-ton block of Portland stone. He had, in 1964, been awarded a top honour for his work on Guildford Cathedral's St Martha of Bethany statue.

On 14th May 1965, the Queen inaugurated Britain's memorial to a 'true and dedicated champion of liberty'.

The ceremony was attended by the widowed Mrs Jacqueline Kennedy and her children, Caroline, 7, and John, 4, together with Lord Harlech, the former British Ambassador to Washington and chairman of the Kennedy Memorial Trustees who in the 1980s, was killed in a car crash.

Mrs Kennedy said at the ceremony: "For free men everywhere, Runnymede is indeed sacred soil. It is the birthplace of our ideals of human freedom and individual dignity in which my husband passionately believed."

Former Prime Minister Harold Macmillan (1957-1963) said: "Every home; every family in Britain felt a sense of personal bereavement. Every household seemed in mourning as though a member of the family had been snatched away."

Harold Wilson, who took over as Prime Minister from Sir A. Douglas-Home in 1964, said of J.F. Kennedy: "Here was a man who brought new hope and vitality to a tired world."

Guildford Cathedral consecrated, May 1961

Wednesday 17th May 1961 was a day of triumph in the life of Guildford Diocese. After 30 years of frustration and anxiety, the Cathedral of the Holy Spirit, Guildford, was consecrated by the new Bishop in the presence of the Queen, Princess Margaret and Mr Antony Armstrong-Jones. The sermon was preached by the Archbishop of Canterbury and the service was one of 'reverence and impressive dignity' according to the *Surrey Advertiser*.

Three times the Bishop with his pastoral staff, knocked from the outside of the west door. "Finally, in almost imperative tones, the Bishop and those with him cried out, 'Open, open open'. The doors were opened and Dr Reindorp was heard saying, 'Peace be to this House'."

Walton Hop – Cricketers Hotel – Co-op Hall – Duke's Head – Staines Town Hall

Bowie at Walton, Clapton at Chertsey

Big names at Chertsey, June 1969.

WHEN bulldozers razed the function room of a Chertsey public house to make way for modern offices, it marked the end of an era.

For the Cricketers, near Chertsey Bridge, was one of the area's top live music venues in the 60s. At the height of the 'beat boom', the little hall hosted the cream of the British R'n'B scene. Here, gyrating crowds danced the night away to shows by Rod Stewart, Fleetwood Mac and Eric Clapton, just to name a few.

The Cricketers' Riverside Club was run by Gortel Promotions of New Haw, whose first booking was the Graham Bond Organisation which boasted Jack Bruce on bass and Ginger Baker on drums, later to join Eric Clapton to form Cream. Other performers included the Zoot Money's Big Roll Band featuring Andy Summers on lead guitar (12 years away from becoming a member of Police); Chris Farlowe; the outrageous Pretty Things plus 18-year-old Mick Fleetwood.

The club also boasted of an appearance by Goldie and the Gingerbreads, the first ever all-girl USA group to actually play their instruments.

Regular club visitors in those heady days also included John Mayall's Bluesbreakers, with a fresh-faced, 20-year-old guitarist from Ripley – Eric Clapton. A huge American blues festival was held in 1965 featuring veteran musician Sonny Boy Williamson. Queues for the show trailed down the street to the Weir Road traffic lights. Four months later, Sonny died in the USA.

In late 1965 the club shut but re-opened in February 1967, run by Gordon Grey. Then, Mick Fleetwood and future Rolling Stone Mick Taylor performed and in September 1967, Rod Stewart filled the clubroom with his inimitable vocals while in the Jeff Beck Group. On bass that night was Ronnie Wood, another future Stone. The same month, Fleetwood Mac made their first appearance. Other acts to play included Ten Years After, Eddie 'knock on wood' Floyd, Jethro Tull, Rory Gallagher and Champion Jack Dupree. Chertsey man Steve Kemp was a regular dj, along with Chris Childs.

When a London promotions firm took over in 1969, newly-popular reggae acts such as Desmond Dekker appeared, but skinheads caused trouble. Thereafter, discos replaced live acts.

Other local concerts included Screaming Lord Sutch at Chertsey Constitutional Hall in 1964 and the Small Faces in 1965. Paul Simon was at the Duke's Head, Addlestone, in 1964. The Strawbs and Peter Sarsted also visited.

Addlestone's Co-op Hall staged gigs by Dave Berry, The Mojos, Applejacks, Amen Corner and the Merseybeats. Individual musicians destined for bigger things also played. These included Jimmy Page, Ronnie Wood, Mick Taylor and Mitch Mitchell (later the drummer with Jimi Hendrix) plus Greg Lake.

The Walton Hop hosted Richie Blackmore (later in Deep Purple); 16-year-old Peter Frampton in The Herd, and the pre-glam rock Sweet. Van Morrison – 'a thin lead singer with a shock of hair' – played with Them and most notable of all, Davy Jones (later David Bowie) appeared in March 1965 while a member of Davy Jones and the Lower Third.

In 1966, the 20-year-old Van Morrison was at Staines Town Hall in a year which saw the Yardbirds, Pretty Things, The Birds in addition to Wayne Fontana and the Mindbenders appear. Wayne 'drew a barrage of screams' when he joined his group on stage, the *Surrey Herald* reported.

continued on page 140

Country town with a community spirit — and The Rex

Haslemere's Espresso a haven for youth

HASLEMERE was already well established as a commuter town by the time the 60s came along, although as the decade progressed, it became even more so.

Set in beautiful countryside, the town had always been popular with those escaping the hurly burly of London but not wanting to be too far away.

More and more senior citizens, merchant bankers and civil servants and the like moved into the area, populating the large attractive houses just outside the town centre in Weydown Road, Beech Road, Hill Road, Bunch Lane and others.

The town retained a lively community atmosphere with bustling shopping centres in the High Street and Wey Hill with a wide choice of shops.

That community togetherness manifested itself when parents of children at the St Bartholomew's Junior School in Chestnut Avenue clubbed together and raised money to pay for a swimming pool at the school, one of the first school pools in the county.

There was also the start of the fund-raising to build an indoor swimming pool for the people of the town, which eventually succeeded and the pool was built in Shottermill.

A fairly conservative town, Haslemere was not awash with beautiful people, mods, rockers, and Mary Quant clothes horses, but they were there if you looked. The haunt of the youth of Haslemere, apart from the numerous pubs that were still open and thriving then, was the Espresso at the bottom of Wey Hill.

A classic coffee bar with the black and white chess board tiles on the floor, wooden chairs and formica tables, the Espresso was a haven for the youth who sat around chatting and laughing over an everlasting coffee or Coke and listening to the hits.

The Rex Cinema, a giant, in Shottermill, was one of the best of its type in the country. Opened in the 30s, it was a classic Art Deco building, seating up to 1,000, and was frequently filled. A huge screen, with plush seats and sweet shop made the Rex a great place for a night out.

Rolf Harris, Joe Brown and Marty Wilde were on the bill at Haslemere's Rex Cinema in January 1963 – the month of the great freeze-up.

Its independent owner-manager, Richard Killinger was able to utilise his extensive contacts in the show-business world to get the biggest and newest films as early as any of the big chains, sometimes opening a blockbuster on the Sunday after its London premiere on the previous Thursday.

The Rex also had a large stage which frequently saw big concerts from classical orchestras to the top pop groups of the day. In fact, the Beatles themselves were due to appear in the early days of their rise to fame but were lured away by the clamour for the fab four in the States and an American tour put paid to their appearance at the Rex. The cinema's life ended in late 1985 and the site was redeveloped with flats.

Live entertainment elsewhere was chiefly provided in the Haslemere Hall in Bridge Road.

Every July, the world renowned Haslemere Festival of ancient music attracted thousands of visitors to the town from many foreign parts including America, Australia and all over Europe. Although such a major part of the British classical music year, the Festival, as it continued to be for many years, was a family affair, run by the Dolmetsch clan.

Something for everybody at the Rex, Haslemere, in February 1963, with a top orchestra, then, a week later, all-star wrestling with Doctor Death, Mike Marino, Black Butcher Johnson and others. Pop groups The Hollies, Bachelors and Freddie and the Dreamers also drew the crowds.

Also at Haslemere Hall were the regular productions by the Haslemere Players presenting musicals and the Haslemere Thespians who put on a wide range of plays. And there was, of course, the hugely popular annual pantomime, all going strong for many years after the 60s.

Worrying headlines from the Surrey Advertiser, March 1963, affecting Elstead.

Bird's nest soup at Hindhead

Less than a decade before the start of the 60s, the Hindhead's Punch Bowl Hotel was a temperance hotel, but there was no such restriction in the Sixties. The many tourists to the beautiful countryside around the Devil's Punchbowl nearby used to stop for a welcome pint at the Punch Bowl.

One curiosity was that in 1964 it served a steaming bird's nest soup, which proved an interesting starter to the main dishes on the menu which included boeuf strogonoff. The hotel had a good reputation for specialising in English cheeses in the 60s.

37 killed as Spanish jet hits hilltop

Plane crashes near Haslemere

Haslemere was the focus of national news on 4th November 1967 when a jet aircraft crashed on Black Down, just half a mile from the Surrey boundary to the south of the town.

The Iberia Caravelle Spanish airliner, travelling from Malaga to London, ploughed into a wooded hilltop in the National Trust countryside thick with trees and populated only by the occasional farmhouse or cottage.

One theory is that the pilot thought he was travelling at a height of 7000 feet, but was, in fact, only 700 feet above sea level – too low to clear the undulating landscape on the Surrey and Sussex boundary near Tennyson's Lane and Fernden Lane, Black Down.

Hordes of journalists headed for Haslemere, some of them staying at the home of a Mr Coles, a market gardener, living near the scene of the crash. As rescue teams clambered up the hillside to discover the full scale of the tragedy, there were reports of nearby villagers going to all lengths to get a glimpse of the carnage. At least one woman wheeled a pushchair over a long stretch of rugged terrain to view the scene.

"I wore a mohair mini to the Ready Steady Go Club."

Diary of Sonia Farley (aged 13¼)

TEENAGERS in their droves used to flock to the Ready Steady Go Club at The Hut, Westcott, in the early Sixties.

The club was named after the cult pop programme on independent television and was a big attraction for fashionable young people from the Westcott, Dorking, Abinger and Wooton areas.

One of those teenagers was Sonia Farley (aged 13 and 3 months) who recalled: "According to my diary entry for 3rd March 1964, I went to the club for the first time on becoming a member. I wore my mohair mini and a polo neck jumper." Sonia was accompanied by her friend Ann Tickner and both lived at Abinger Common in the council's Evelyn Cottages.

"It was called the Ready Steady Go Club but when you were really flash, you called it the RSG Club. There seemed to be no age limit. There was no alcohol or any food or drinks for sale. We had to go to the club next door for Coke and crisps."

Bands used to play at the Hut and sometimes, chart acts performed. These included Heinz and later, Harmony Grass who used their earlier name of Tony Rivers and the Castaways even though they were in the hit parade with 'Move A Little Closer'.

Here is a peep at some of the entries Sonia made in her diary in the first part of 1964.

Saturday 8th February 1964: "Went into the Flicks (at Dorking). Managed to get into an 'A' on my own. A boy called Geoff Wood came and sat next to me. He wore leather jeans and a leather jacket."

Wednesday 12th February 1964: "Beatlemania has struck the USA. The girls over there are begging them to stay but I won't let them."

Friday 14th February 1964: "Met Chris Pople outside Woolworth's (in Dorking) and went with her to South Holmwood. We had fish and chips there and went to a Valentines dance in the village hall. It was smashing. There were two groups, Tommy and the Peddlers who are fab and another called The Sects. It was just like the Ready Steady Go Club. About 200 people all under the age of 21."

Saturday 22nd February 1964: "Tidied my room and listened to the transistor. The Beatles were on and later they were on the telly. The Beatles were in a studio and the roofs of cars were smashed in,

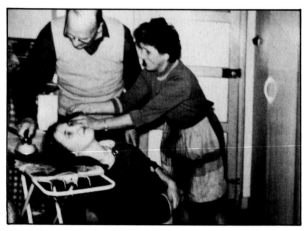

Sonia has her hair ironed between brown paper by an uncle.

iron barriers crushed beyond repair and lots of girls fainted."

Sunday 23rd February 1964: Tonibell man came round the estate and had a puncture. I am daft. I gave two shillings to Ron to get me some tickets for a Valentines dance at the Ready Steady Go Club. I watched The Saint on TV. I hope to go ice skating at Richmond on Saturday."

Monday 25th February 1964: "Ron came on a motorbike. He said he could not get the tickets. We got the bus to Westcott and wandered around the outside but we did not dare to go in. Cassius Clay won a fight against Sonny Liston. I bought a jar of Pond's cold cream."

Tuesday 3rd March 1964: "Went to the Ready Steady Go Club with Ann. Met two boys who danced with us. I liked the one who danced with Ann the best. They were dressed in suits and looked smart. Got my Ready Steady Go membership card number 1643. Three shillings left for the flicks on Saturday."

Wednesday 4th March 1964: "Wore my hair in the style of the Ronettes at school today."

Tuesday 7th April 1964: "Ann found that we could get Radio Caroline on our transistor. It's something like Luxemburg but we could not hear it very well."

Sonia also had a vivid memory of walking down her road in summer when people had all their windows open. All along the street she could hear the sound of the Z-cars' theme tune.

Twinkle, Twinkle, little star

Twinkle aged 16 and her hit record on Decca.
Inset: Twinkle's father, Alderman Sydney Ripley,
Surrey County Council chairman in the early 60s.

Lynn Ripley, 12, (later pop star Twinkle) presents
the Queen with flowers on her visit to Kingston.

Queen visits Kingston
— Jagger fights over Lynn

THE Queen came to historic Kingston in March 1961. On the sunny afternoon of Thursday 24th, she arrived, wearing a cherry red coat and over the next two hours, captivated the town and its people with her charm and interest in everything she saw.

Her Royal Highness came to mark the 400th anniversary of the granting of a charter by Elizabeth I to Kingston Grammar School but she also made an official visit to County Hall, headquarters of Surrey County Council, where she was handed a bouquet by 12-year-old Lynn Ripley, daughter of Alderman Sydney Ripley, chairman of the County Council. This cute Kingston schoolgirl, less than four years later, was to become a blonde pop star.

Under the name of Twinkle, she climbed the charts to number four with the haunting song, Terry, about a motorcycle rider who crashed and lost his life. Twinkle wrote the song herself but it was nearly banned from the Light channel on the wireless because it was deemed to be in poor taste.

She became record label colleagues with the Rolling Stones and toured with them. On a plane coming back from Ireland, Brian Jones, the Stone who died in the swimming pool, was sitting next to her on the aircraft. Suddenly, Mick Jagger became jealous and ordered Jones to move out of the way. Twinkle decided to stay put; Mick glared at Jones and sauntered off.

Her parents were always concerned about the casual sex problem in the Sixties and therefore employed a nanny to travel with her when she toured with bands. The Stones only kissed her, she said.

Motorists stop for a warming winter drink in Ye Olde Whyte Harte Hotel in Bletchingley, between Redhill and Oxted during a cold spell in the early part of the decade. The inn was first documented as being a public house in 1388. In the Sixties, the pub's beer mats had the village name Bletchingley spelt two ways – one with the 't' and one without to keep locals satisfied, since an argument existed as to the correct spelling of the village name. "The postal address is definitely with a 't', yet the post office opposite proudly proclaimed itself as being that of 'Blechingley'," one observer said at the time.

Redhill man in Status Quo

In the mid Sixties, Redhill band Side Kicks had a guitarist, Roy Lynes who later went on to join Status Quo at the time Quo's first chart hit, Pictures of Matchstick Men on the Pye label, reached number seven in February 1968. The line-up of Side Kicks in the picture above is, from left to right, Roy Lynes (of the Upper Bridge Road area of Redhill); Mick Crunden, Otto Hill and Johnny Wicks.

Winklepickers used as brakes

continued from page 135

All over Surrey, there was a tidal wave in the popularity of Sixties music. At Guildford Odeon, one fan swept up in the excitement, smashed the dressing room window with her fist after Brian Hyland appeared and was signing autographs. Nearby, regular scenes included mods buzzing down the town centre on their motorbikes using their worn-out shoes as brakes. One lad, on a Vincent, "reached 100mph", braking with the soles of his winklepickers near the Railway Cafe. There were often scuffles between youths. One, called Badger, 'could fight his way out of anywhere'.

Saturday nights sometimes saw a fracas at Guildford Bus Station, and on one occasion, Badger threw one of the troublemakers into the river, according to a fellow teenager, Jackie Everett. The Seven Stars in Swan Lane was a popular haunt of firstly teds, then mods and rockers who often clashed. Two local musicians at that time were Philip Goodhand-Tait and John Renbourne, who both attended Pewley School.

The Heralds' better half from the Kingston upon Thames Lambretta Club, 1960.

Members prepare for their autumn rally in 1960. The group met at the Albert Hotel, Kingston Hill, and was the first club of its kind in the country. Rallies were held at night-time as well as during the day. "It was brilliant – great fun", reminisced member Roger Swan.

The Kingston scooter riders enjoy a Sunday run to Epsom Downs in 1960.

Index to towns and villages

Traffic-free – Brighton Road, Burgh Heath c. 1960.

Index to towns and villages

Burgh Heath junction c. 1960 with a small parade of shops, including a barber's on the right.

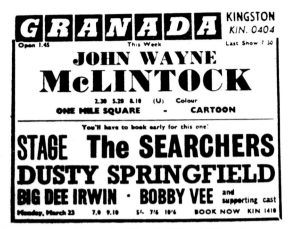

A pop extravaganza in March 1964 at Kingston Granada.

Snow is brushed off a Croydon Times van in the 1962-3 winter.

About the authors

MARK Davison has chronicled everyday life and events in Surrey since his 1960s childhood days when he kept a daily diary at Hook near Kingston and saved up all his Saturday sixpences to subscribe to the *Fabulous* pop magazine. He was soon singing the praises of Dusty Springfield, the Supremes and the Ronettes and each week cut out the top thirty from the daily papers.

In later life, he worked as a journalist on the Kingston Borough News, Surrey Mirror, Banstead Herald, Epsom Herald and East Grinstead Observer. His rock and pop column, Offbeat, has been widely read by Surrey's young people for several years.

He is also interested in local history and climate. Together with Ian Currie he has written the Surrey Weather book and Surrey In the Hurricane – a souvenir book on the great storm of October 1987, plus other county weather books.

He has also dabbled in dee-jaying at Dorking where, as Motown Mark, he presented an evening of 60s Motown music on Monday nights.

Mark has lived in Reigate for several years.

IAN Currie was given a special Christmas present in 1962 – a weather station. He had just got it set up on Boxing Day when it became buried under a heavy blanket of snow which lay on the ground until early March.

His interest in the weather past and present has grown over the years and he is now an expert 'weather historian' – able to recall whether it rained or shined in any year over the past century and beyond.

Before moving to Rickman Hill, Coulsdon, in 1979, he resided at Wallington for a time. For 13 years he taught in Caterham. He has two sons and his wife is a teacher in Croydon.

Ian is a member of the Croydon Natural History and Scientific Society and is in charge of their weather section.

He often gives illustrated talks to clubs and historical societies on past weather and is only too keen to expound on the fascinating weather of the 1960s.

Ian is the weather columnist on the Surrey Comet, Epsom Herald and Surrey Mirror Series and predicted the 1987 great storm with accuracy.

Other titles by the same authors

Surrey In The Seventies (ISBN 0-9516710-7-3). Price £9.95. Published by Frosted Earth.
The Surrey Weather Book (ISBN 0-9516710-3-0). Price £9.95. Published by Frosted Earth.
Red Sky At Night – Weather Sayings For All Seasons (ISBN 0-9516710-2-2). Price £4.95. Published by Frosted Earth.
Surrey In The Hurricane (ISBN 0-9513019-2-6). Price £7.50. Published by Froglets.
London's Hurricane (ISBN 0-9513019-3-4). Price £7.95.
Surrey Street, Croydon – 100 years of market trading by Vivien Lovett (ISBN 0-951671-5-7). Published by Frosted Earth.
Frosts, Freezes And Fairs (ISBN 0-9516710-8-1). Price £8.95. Published by Frosted Earth.